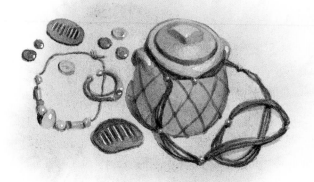

SECRETS
of the PAST

SECRETS of the PAST

A Supplement to
Childcraft—The How and Why Library

World Book, Inc.
a Scott Fetzer company
Chicago

Acknowledgments

"A Mummy Walking in the Crypt" and "The Reason Skeletons Don't Wear Clothes" from *Two Skeletons on the Telephone and Other Poems from Tough City*. Text copyright © 1992 by Paul Duggan. Illustration copyright © 1992 by Daniel Sylvestre. Reprinted by permission of The Millbrook Press and Raincoast Books. All rights reserved.

"Galleon" and "Skeleton Key" from *Keepers* (Lothrop, Lee & Shepard) by Alice Schertle, copyright © 1996 by Alice Schertle. Used by permission of the author, who controls all rights.

I Am the Mummy Heb-Nefert excerpts and illustration. Text copyright © 1997 by Eve Bunting. Illustration copyright © 1997 by David Christiana. By permission of Harcourt, Inc.

For information about other World Book publications, visit our Web site http://www.worldbook.com, or call 1-800-WORLDBK (967-5325). For information about sales to schools and libraries, call: 1-800-975-3250 (United States); 1-800-837-5365 (Canada).

World Book, Inc.
233 North Michigan Avenue
Chicago, IL 60601
U.S.A.

Library of Congress Cataloging-in-Publication Data

Secrets of the past: a supplement to Childcraft—the how and why library.
    p. cm.
    Summary: Junior archaeologists explain what archaeology is and how archaeologists work in different environments around the world, as well as what their findings can tell us about different cultures. Includes activities.
    Includes bibliographical references and index.
    ISBN 0-7166-0602-X
    1. Archaeology—Juvenile literature. 2. Antiquities—Juvenile literature. 3. Historic sites—Juvenile literature. 4. Excavations (Archaeology)—Juvenile literature. [1. Archaeology. 2. Antiquities. 3. Historic sites. 4. Excavations (Archaeology)] I. World Book, Inc. II. Childcraft annual.
CC171.S43 2002
930.1—dc21
                                                                        2002016766

Printed in the United States of America

1 2 3 4 5 6 7 8 9 10 11 10 09 08 07 06 05 04 03 02

STAFF

TABLE of CONTENTS

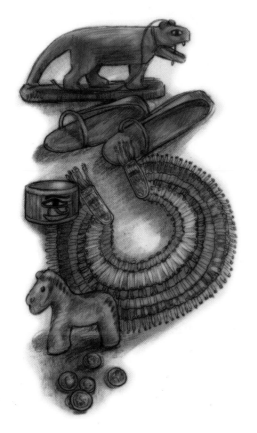

DISCOVERING IN JUNGLES AND CAVES 136

DISCOVERING UNDERWATER 172

PREFACE

Have you ever watched an adventure movie about mummies, tomb raiders, or temples of doom? Well, there is more to archaeology, and it's all here in the action-packed **Secrets of the Past.**

In this book, you will join junior archaeologists as they learn what the professionals do. You will visit deserts, mountaintops, jungles, caves, and underwater ruins. But not all discoveries are found in faraway places. Read the **Closer to Homes** features and you may learn about an exciting discovery made in a city near you! Check out the **Dig Even Deeper** features to find fun ways that you can dig into archaeology at home.

At the back of the book are resources to help with your explorations. The **Secrets of the Past Chronology** lets you view discoveries on a timeline. To read about a certain part of the world, look at the **Secrets of the Past World Map.** Turn to the **Glossary** to understand difficult terms that you come across. The **Index** will help you quickly find a subject in this book. Your parents and teachers can use **Find Out More** to select other books and Web sites about archaeology.

Now, turn the page to start uncovering **Secrets of the Past!**

ARCHAEOLOGISTS *as* DETECTIVES

I HOPE YOU CAN HELP ME. I FOUND THIS BURIED BEHIND MY HOUSE, AND I HAVE NO IDEA WHAT IT IS!

THAT'S OUR JOB! WE ARCHAEOLOGISTS ARE TIME DETECTIVES. WE LOVE INVESTIGATING THINGS THAT BELONGED TO PEOPLE WHO LIVED IN THE PAST.

Ancient objects can be classified into two groups—artifacts and ecofacts. Artifacts are objects that were made, used, or changed by people. Tools, jewelry, and statues are good examples of artifacts. So are tombstones and parts of old buildings. Ecofacts include things left over from cooking, such as seeds and animal bones, as well as other things that originally came from the environment.

Sometimes ecofacts are found along with artifacts or in the ruins of structures built by people of the past.

Artifacts and ecofacts are important to archaeologists (AHR kee AHL uh jihsts). Archaeologists look for clues about the lives of people who lived in the past and people whose cultures no longer exist.

Artifacts and ecofacts are especially important to archaeologists who look for clues about the lives of prehistoric people, people who lived before the invention of writing. These people began making things like tools nearly $2\frac{1}{2}$ million years before anyone even thought of recording information on stone or clay. Studying artifacts and ecofacts from the places where prehistoric people lived, worked, or were buried is the only way to learn about their way of life. Artifacts and ecofacts tell us about their art and beliefs, their customs and values.

Some archaeologists also study the writings people left behind. People who wrote and read were

DIG EVEN DEEPER...
ARTIFACTS YOU LIVE WITH

Look for old appliances, furniture, or tools in your kitchen, attic, or garage. What is the oldest thing in your home? Where did it come from? How is it used? Do you still use it today? Or do you use a different object to do the same job?

IF YOU HAVE WRITTEN RECORDS OF PEOPLE, WHY DO ARCHAEOLOGISTS BOTHER TO STUDY THE THINGS THESE PEOPLE LEFT BEHIND?

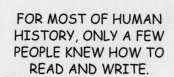

FOR MOST OF HUMAN HISTORY, ONLY A FEW PEOPLE KNEW HOW TO READ AND WRITE.

SUPPOSE YOUR DIARY WAS THE ONLY WRITTEN RECORD WE HAD ABOUT THE LIVES OF ALL THE STUDENTS IN YOUR SCHOOL. WHAT WOULD YOU WANT TO INCLUDE?

usually wealthy and powerful. As a result, ancient writings tell us very little about the daily lives of ordinary people.

Up until the 1400's, most writing in Europe and Asia was done by scribes (skrybz). Scribes were people trained to write letters or books by hand for others. They recorded laws, tax records, and other government documents. They also wrote business contracts, records of land sales, and religious writings.

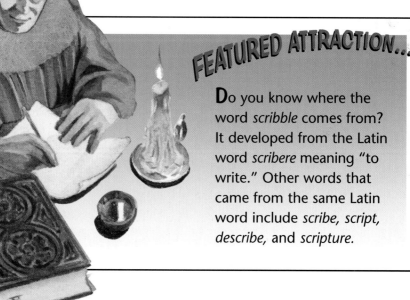

FEATURED ATTRACTION...

Do you know where the word *scribble* comes from? It developed from the Latin word *scribere* meaning "to write." Other words that came from the same Latin word include *scribe, script, describe,* and *scripture.*

This artifact is a clay model of a chariot. It was made in the ancient region of Mesopotamia about 1600-1900 B.C.

This squash seed is an ecofact. It was found in Mexico and is about 9,000 years old.

Artifacts and ecofacts that archaeologists find tell us about the lives of all types of people. They help us learn how a particular culture (KUHL chuhr)— a certain way of life—developed and how that culture changed over time. In some cases, they help us understand when and why that culture died out.

Where are artifacts and ecofacts found? Many are found in the ancient ruins of houses or temples. They are also found in ancient graves. But the best place to look for ecofacts is in heaps of garbage that have grown over time. In the past, people threw out their food wastes and other trash right where they lived, and the garbage piled up. These piles are called middens. Many ecofacts—and often artifacts, too—lie undisturbed in middens until someone digs them up.

One of the most important things archaeologists learn from an artifact or ecofact is its age. Knowing the age of an object gives a clue about the age of the site (syt)—place— where it was found. It may also tell us the age of other things found with it. Some artifacts, such as coins, are marked with the date when they were made. The ages of other artifacts are harder to figure out. Ecofacts usually need to be tested in a laboratory to find their age.

SO WHAT CAN YOU LEARN FROM ARTIFACTS AND ECOFACTS?

Artifacts and ecofacts can also help identify the people who used them. Suppose the animal parts found in the midden behind an ancient house came mainly from the heads, tails, or feet of pigs. This could suggest that the people might have cooked these parts because of some religious beliefs. In another midden, the garbage might include the seeds of rare imported spices. This would tell an archaeologist that the people who lived there probably traded with other people who lived far away. But good archaeologists never draw conclusions from only one piece of evidence. They build a case based on many artifacts and bits of information.

This flute was carved from the wing bone of a crane. The flute was found in a grave at an ancient farming community in the Yellow River Valley in China. It may be up to 9,000 years old.

LOOK AT WHAT IS LYING AROUND MY OFFICE, AND YOU CAN SEE FOR YOURSELF HOW PILES OF DISCARDED THINGS TALK!

THE BANANA PEEL IS A CLUE TO WHAT I LIKE TO EAT. THE WORN-OUT SOCK TELLS YOU SOMETHING ABOUT HOW I DRESS. THE TICKET STUB FROM THE MOVIE GIVES YOU SOME IDEA OF WHAT I LIKE TO DO IN MY SPARE TIME.

Artifacts can help archaeologists learn what people did for a living—or for fun. Lumps of dried clay, smashed pots, kilns, and pottery wheels found at a site suggest that the people who lived there made pottery. A box with squares on the top and small tokens inside suggests that the people who lived at a site enjoyed board games. A thin wooden tube with holes in it might tell us that someone once played flutelike music.

People in the ancient city of Ur, in southwestern Asia, made this game thousands of years ago. The playing pieces were made from shells and a stone called lapiz lazuli.

17

FINDS From PRIVIES

Middens, or garbage heaps, may seem like strange places to find clues to the past, but here's one place that seems even more unusual—the bathroom! Imagine what people might learn about you by looking at the things in YOUR bathroom.

For most of human history, people did not have tiled bathrooms and flush toilets. One type of early toilet was the privy (PRIHV ee). Some privies were simply small buildings containing a bench with holes built over a deep pit. They were often built just outside the house. Other privies were simply holes in the ground, usually covered by a small building. Luckily for archaeologists, privies often served as garbage pits, too. Archaeologists have dug up many kinds of privies in cities and towns.

Privies have been great at preserving material. New deposits of human waste rapidly covered older deposits. This prevented buried items from decomposing—decaying. From the material found in a privy, archaeologists can find out what the people who used it ate and drank. By testing human wastes, which privy diggers call night soil, archaeologists can even tell if the people had diseases and which medicines they took.

A privy's contents may also include kitchen scraps, bones, seeds, window glass, and pieces of pottery or porcelain. Medicine bottles, pipes, coins, marbles, doll parts, shells from guns, old tools, pot lids, locks, and of course, chamber pots—portable toilets—have also been found in privies.

Do you think archaeologists in the future will be able to view your wastes as easily? That is not likely, because most people do not dump their garbage outside their back door today. In most cities and towns, garbage trucks pick up trash from people's homes and take it to dumps far away. There, the trash is buried or burned. Toilets are now part of huge sewer systems that carry human waste to treatment plants.

DIG EVEN DEEPER... WASTES NOT WASTED

Do you think this ancient mammoth waste might be helpful to archaeologists? You bet! Archaeologists learn a lot from wastes left behind by animals. Often, such wastes are found dried at excavation sites. By testing the remains, archaeologists can learn about an ancient environment, the plants and animals that once lived there, and how people tended their animals.

By looking at the remains of this public bathroom that was used in ancient Rome, archaeologists can learn about ancient architecture.

19

Making ARTIFACTS TALK

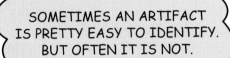

SOMETIMES AN ARTIFACT IS PRETTY EASY TO IDENTIFY. BUT OFTEN IT IS NOT.

"**M**any artifacts are difficult to identify," explained Jack, an archaeologist." An artifact may have been broken, and we cannot find all the pieces. Or sometimes, an object just does not look like anything we use nowadays. Look at the artifact that I am holding. Can you figure out what it is?"

"It seems to be pottery," said Zach, intent on learning more about archaeology. "That means it was made of baked clay. There is no bone, wood, stone, fabric, paper, or plastic on it."

"Good. What else do you notice about it?" asked Jack.

"It has a lot of cracks in it. I would guess it is pretty old," Zach replied.

"It is! By looking at the age of some of the items that were found around it,

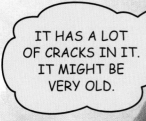

IT HAS A LOT
OF CRACKS IN IT.
IT MIGHT BE
VERY OLD.

we figure that it is about 2,500 years old,"
said Jack. "Anything else?"

"It does not have any writing on it to tell
me what it is, when it was made, or who might
have owned it," said Zach.

"Right again. It doesn't even have a design,"
added Jack. "Sometimes the decorations on an
artifact are a clue. They help us identify the
group of people who made the object. Does it
look like anything you have ever seen before?"

"It looks a lot like a bowl with two handles,"
said Zach. "Was it used for cooking or serving
food?"

"Nope. But don't feel bad. Sometimes it takes
a lot of archaeologists and a lot of time to
figure out what an artifact is. And then we may
find out that our first theory was wrong! Do
you notice anything unusual about this
mysterious artifact?" asked Jack.

"Now that you mention it," replied Zach,
"I can see a strange little hole at the bottom.
I know—it is an ancient water cooler."

"You are getting warmer. It was used to hold
water, but not for drinking," Jack explained.

"I give up. What is it?" asked Zach.

"It is an ancient Greek water clock," Jack announced. "Most people in ancient Greece used sundials to tell time. But on cloudy days, at night, or indoors, Greeks used water clocks— jars filled with water. A wooden stick floated upright in the water. As the water drained out through the hole in the bottom, marks on the sinking stick showed how much time had

These people are looking for artifacts and ecofacts at a site in Epidaurus, in southwestern Greece. The people who lived here long ago might have used a water clock to mark time.

passed. Because the stick was wooden, it rotted away, leaving only the pot for us to uncover. Now you can see why our job takes so much detective work. When we do not have all the evidence, we have to do a lot of guesswork to get a complete picture."

"Very cool. But I think the clock on my nightstand is a lot easier to read—and its parts are made to last, too!"

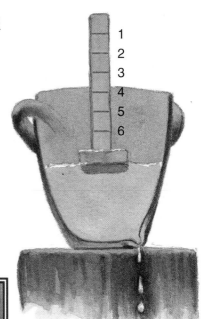

The ancient Greeks used a variety of styles of water clocks. Some had markings on the inside. Some had a floating device, like a wooden rod, that marked the hours. This type of clock may have served more as a timer than a timepiece, because the hours were marked in descending order. The Greeks probably used this style to time the length of orators' speeches.

LOST and FOUND

Think of something you have lost or thrown away recently, such as a broken yo-yo, toothbrush, sunglasses, or tennis racket. Imagine that someone has found this item a few hundred years in the future. Do you think that person would know what the object is? Would the item still be sold in stores? Would the person know how it should be used?

Now imagine that the person who has found the item has given it to a museum. The museum is putting together a display of artifacts from the early 2000's. Each item will have a sign giving its name and explaining how it was used. Make up a sign for your chosen item.

What: <Put the name of the object here.>

When: <Put the approximate date it was last used here.>

How: <Tell how the object was used and whether it is still used. If it is not used, why?>

The following signs will accompany other items in the display. You can use these as models for your sign.

If you cannot think of anything to describe, try creating a museum card for a CD-ROM, DVD, in-line skates, or a handheld computer game.

What: a potato peeler

When: last used in the 2010's

How: People used this device to peel potatoes, as well as other vegetables and fruits. This was before scientists developed produce with skins that pop off with a twist of the wrist.

What: a videocassette

When: last used in the 2010's

How: Today, we can call up and watch our favorite movies on our three-dimensional computer or television. In the past however, people used to rent or buy these plastic cases, which held a thin tape. People would put the case into a machine to watch a taped movie on an old-fashioned two-dimensional television.

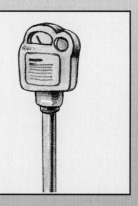

What: a parking meter

When: last used in the 2030's

How: People once were allowed to drive their cars to downtown areas of cities and park there on the streets, if they paid a small amount of money into this machine.

Then and NOW

"This place is full of stuff from a zillion years ago!" Jack said to Clare when they entered the museum. "Coming here is like visiting another planet."

Clare gave Jack a disapproving look. "I disagree, but, of course, that is why we are here. My hypothesis (hy POTH uh sihs) for our archaeology project is: Modern people have a lot in common with ancient people."

"No way!" insisted Jack. "The people who used these artifacts did not have televisions or computers or even cars. I do not think the things they made and used mean anything to modern kids like us."

"Well, that is definitely a doll," Clare said, while pointing at the display case. "It even has

The woven papyrus sandals above are from Egypt's New Kingdom, about 1554 B.C. Rubber flip-flops like the ones at the right are more common nowadays.

The Egyptian wig above was made from human hair about 1550-1300 B.C. Today, many people wear wigs made of human and artificial hair, like the one shown below.

joints in its shoulders and hips, like my old Barbie dolls."

"Hmm. And that chair does look like the ones in our dining room," Jack said.

"And here is something that looks familiar," Clare said, pointing to a display of Asian artifacts.

Jack looked down at Clare's feet, "OK, OK, they look like your flip-flops. But yours are made of rubber and these are woven from some kind of reed."

"Wait!" Jack said happily. "Check this out. I bet you don't know what this is!"

"It's very pretty, whatever it is," said Clare, with a puzzled look. "Maybe it is some sort of necklace or wall decoration."

"Wrong," Jack grinned. "It's a wig. I'll bet you have never seen anyone wearing anything like it."

"True," Clare admitted. "But a lot of people today wear wigs. The idea has not changed, just the style and the material."

"Let's check out the displays on Europe," said Jack.

Ancient Irish razor made of bronze

"Sure," said Clare. "Why this old French pottery is similar to pottery pitchers made today. And this coin reminds me of that quarter you owe me."

"Hey, what do you think this weird thing is?" asked Jack, changing the subject.

"It is very small, only about an inch long," said Clare with a sigh. "Maybe it is a miniature vegetable chopper."

"The sign says it is an Irish razor from the A.D. 700's," Jack read. "Irish men used razors like this to trim their beards and mustaches. It sure does not look like the razor my dad uses."

"The razor might look different from razors today, but men still use razors to trim their beards and mustaches," said Clare.

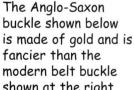
The Anglo-Saxon buckle shown below is made of gold and is fancier than the modern belt buckle shown at the right.

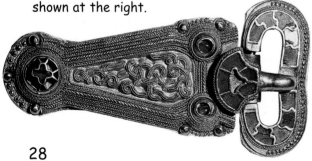

This modern woolen shirt from the United States is not that different from the shirt shown at the left.

This is a girl's woolen shirt, skirt, and belt made in Denmark about 300 B.C.

The pottery cooking utensils at the right were made in France about 3500 B.C. They were as helpful to people as modern pottery pitchers like the one below.

"I guess so," Jack laughed. "It is amazing to me that so many of these old artifacts look like things we use today, or were used for the same purpose as things we use."

"Yep," agreed Clare. "People always need tools to cook and carry food, things to clothe and clean themselves with, and items to amuse themselves, too."

Above left is a Celtic gold coin from the first century A.D. It has a horse on it. Above is a modern U.S. quarter. It shows President George Washington's profile and is made of copper and nickel.

IN THE SPOTLIGHT...

Heinrich Schliemann, shown here at the site of Troy, was a German pioneer in archaeology. He once said that his fascination with the ancient city of Troy began shortly after he turned 8, when his father gave him a book of Greek and Roman myths. One story told of a Trojan War and Troy in flames. Later in life, he set out to prove there actually was a Trojan War. He and his wife, Sophia, conducted the first major excavation of the buried city of Troy in what is now Turkey. Guided by the Greek epic the *Iliad*, they began excavating in 1870. The first artifacts they found there were three gold earrings and a pin. Though the Schliemanns found the famous Troy, they never proved there actually was a Trojan War.

Heinrich
SCHLIEMANN
EXCAVATOR of TROY

DIG EVEN DEEPER...
CREATE YOUR OWN ARTIFACT

Coins are artifacts that tell archaeologists a great deal of information. They may include images of plants, animals, gods, or people. More importantly, they may include a date! You can create a coin artifact that a future archaeologist may find.

YOU WILL NEED

- polymer clay (from craft or hobby store)
- rolling pin or clean hands
- empty film canister or clean top from old milk bottle
- white pencil, sharpened
- paintbrushes and many colors of paint, or permanent markers (get permission first)

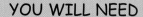

1. Flatten a small ball of clay to $\frac{1}{2}$-inch thickness, using a rolling pin or the palm of your hand.

2. Use the film canister or bottle top like a cookie cutter to cut circles from the flattened clay.

3. Gently carve a design on your coins with the pencil. Draw your face, pet, name, or house. Look at historical coins for other ideas. Be sure to include the date!

4. Ask an adult to help you bake your coins in an ordinary oven according to the directions on the package of clay.

5. When the coins are cool, paint them or color them with permanent marker.

31

OTHER DETECTIVES ON THE SCENE

Here are descriptions of artifacts from different sites. Do you know what they are and how old they are? To learn more about their findings, archaeologists often call in scientists who specialize in one type of artifact or ecofact. Read each of the following six descriptions. Then decide which expert on page 33 should be called in to help. The answers are on page 34.

1. In a midden in New Mexico, an archaeologist has found pieces of bowls unlike the other pieces found there. One has mosquitoes painted on it. Where did these bowls come from?

2. Pollen—a powder from flowers—was scattered over prehistoric bones buried in Iraq. What kind of flowers did the pollen come from?

3. A bronze coin found in London shows the picture of a Roman emperor— but no date. When might the coin have been made?

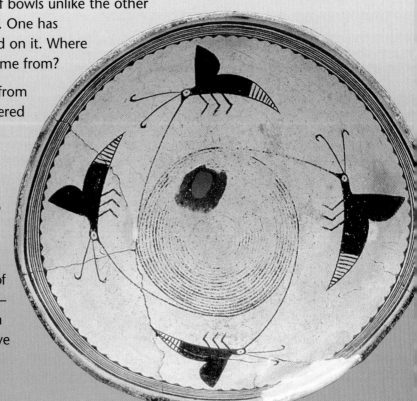

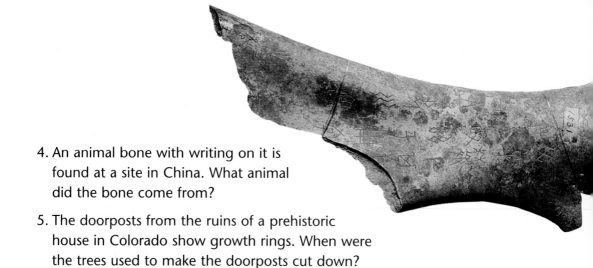

4. An animal bone with writing on it is found at a site in China. What animal did the bone come from?

5. The doorposts from the ruins of a prehistoric house in Colorado show growth rings. When were the trees used to make the doorposts cut down?

6. An archaeologist finds a crooked human leg bone in a burial mound. Did the defect result from injury or disease?

A numismatist

B dendrochronologist

C bioarchaeologist

D archaeozoologist

E archaeobotanist

F ceramic technologist

ANSWERS

1-F A ceramic (suh RAM ihk) technologist studies the shapes and uses of pottery, and its design and decoration, and learns what the information means in different cultures at different times.

2-E An archaeobotanist (AHR kee oh BAHT uhn ihst) studies ancient plant remains and fossils.

3-A A numismatist (noo MIHZ muh tihst) studies coins.

4-D An archaeozoologist (AHR kee oh ZOH ahl uh jihst) studies ancient animals to learn about people's diets, living environment, and economic status.

5-B A dendrochronologist (DEHN droh kruh NAHL uh jihst) studies tree rings to find out the age of wood.

6-C A bioarchaeologist (BY oh AHR kee AHL uh jihst) studies human remains to help determine the life span, diet, health, and diseases of people of the past.

WE NEED YOUR HELP ANALYZING ARTIFACTS AND ECOFACTS!

YOU CALLED THE RIGHT PLACE!

FEATURED ATTRACTION...

Archaeologists have skills that are helpful even in times of disaster. For example, archaeologists have helped authorities recover human remains from conflicts in places such as Bosnia, Cambodia, Korea, Laos, and Vietnam. And in 2001, archaeologists quickly volunteered their services after the World Trade Center towers in New York City were destroyed. Archaeologists are experts in recovering material and human remains. DNA specialists and other specialists know how to help in the identification of victims. Preservationists know how to evaluate the disaster's effect on historic buildings in the area.

Galleon

She rests upon her starboard side.
Little silver fishes slide
between her ribs, and in her hold,
where tentacles embrace her gold,
a curious current gently stirs
the round white bones of mariners.

—by Alice Schertle

Many artifacts sit on the bottom of the sea. Once they may have been part of a massive load carried by a galleon, a large fighter ship. This poem talks about a sunken galleon and how she and her treasures wait to be found.

DISCOVERING THE...

HOW DOES *the* PAST *Get* BURIED?

ARCHAEOLOGISTS FIND EVIDENCE OF THE PAST BENEATH THE EARTH'S DESERT SANDS AND JUNGLES, DEEP IN ITS CAVES, HIGH ON ITS MOUNTAINS, AND EVEN ON ITS OCEAN FLOOR. SO HOW DOES THE PAST GET BURIED?

SOMETIMES A NATURAL DISASTER, SUCH AS AN EARTHQUAKE OR A VOLCANIC ERUPTION, BURIES A CITY OR SETTLEMENT. THE VIOLENT ERUPTION OF VESUVIUS, A MOUNTAIN IN ITALY, IN A.D. 79 RANKS AS ONE OF THE MOST FAMOUS EXAMPLES. THAT ERUPTION BURIED THE ANCIENT ROMAN TOWNS OF POMPEII AND HERCULANEUM. THOUSANDS OF PEOPLE DIED. BUT THE ASH, DUST, AND MUD THAT COVERED THE TOWNS ALSO PRESERVED MANY ARTIFACTS—EVEN THINGS THAT USUALLY DECAY QUICKLY. FOR EXAMPLE, ARCHAEOLOGISTS FOUND ROCK-HARD LOAVES OF BREAD, SOME STAMPED WITH THE BAKER'S INITIALS!

Today, visitors to Pompeii and Herculaneum can see impressions of some of the volcano's victims. Their bodies decayed as the ash and mud that buried them hardened to rock. Eventually, all that remained were hollow spaces in the shapes of the bodies. Archaeologists created casts of the victims by pouring plaster into these spaces and then extracting the molds of the bodies, as shown here.

THE PAST CAN ALSO BE BURIED AT SEA. DANGEROUS WAVES AND A BAD STORM CAN SINK A SHIP.

PEOPLE PLAY A PART IN COVERING UP HISTORY, TOO. SOMETIMES, INVADERS BURN OR BOMBARD A CITY. AFTERWARD, THE INVADERS, OR EVEN THE ORIGINAL INHABITANTS, REBUILD OVER THE RUINS.

WHEN PEOPLE BUILD OVER A SITE AGAIN AND AGAIN, THE LANDSCAPE MAY EVENTUALLY FORM A MOUND. ARCHAEOLOGISTS USUALLY CALL THESE MOUNDS *TELLS. TELL* IS AN ARABIC WORD MEANING "HILL." BY DIGGING IN A *TELL,* ARCHAEOLOGISTS CAN DISCOVER WHO LIVED AT THE SITE OVER THE YEARS.

USUALLY, THE PAST IS BURIED SLOWLY. PEOPLE LEAVE A CERTAIN PLACE IN SEARCH OF SAFETY, FOOD, OR MONEY. OVER TIME, WIND, RAIN, AND ICE WEAR AWAY THE BUILDINGS AND OTHER STRUCTURES LEFT BEHIND. SAND OR DIRT LEVELS THE LANDSCAPE, AND PLANTS BEGIN TO GROW. OR, PEOPLE PLANT CROPS WHERE SETTLEMENTS ONCE STOOD. PEOPLE ALSO BUILD ROADS AND SHOPPING CENTERS OVER THE BURIED REMAINS OF STRUCTURES.

OVER CENTURIES, RIVERBANKS FLOOD. THE WATER DROPS THE SOIL IT IS CARRYING. THE SOIL COVERS THE LAND AND ANY ARTIFACTS AND ECOFACTS THAT MAY BE THERE.

WHERE *Do* ARCHAEOLOGISTS DIG?

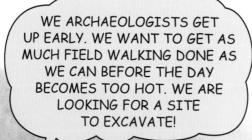

WE ARCHAEOLOGISTS GET UP EARLY. WE WANT TO GET AS MUCH FIELD WALKING DONE AS WE CAN BEFORE THE DAY BECOMES TOO HOT. WE ARE LOOKING FOR A SITE TO EXCAVATE!

A farmer found a couple artifacts in his field. Archaeologists suspect that they are from a group that settled near here long ago. Today, a crew is surveying the land to see if it's likely to have more clues about ancient people who lived here.

The archaeologists walk in a straight line across the field, looking for artifacts and other clues. They walk several feet, then stop and examine the soil. A change in the color of the soil may be all that remains of an old shelter.

An archaeologist pushes a long hollow tube called an auger (AW guhr) into the ground. When he pulls up the tube, it is full of soil. Another uses a shovel to dig up some soil.

The researchers work slowly and carefully. They do not want to miss even the smallest clue. And they do not want to damage anything. They write down their findings as they go.

Sometimes, photographs taken from an airplane or satellite reveal unsuspected sites that cannot be seen from the ground. A bumpy surface, for example, may be a sign that ancient walls or roads are buried there. This aerial photo shows the outlines of a royal Celtic monument in Ireland that dates from about 2000 B.C.

Instruments that send out radio waves or radar waves help archaeologists "see" underground. The waves go down into the ground. If the waves hit an object, they bounce back to the instrument. By figuring out how long it takes the echoes of the waves to return, archaeologists know how far underground the object is. The pattern the echoes make on the viewing screen helps tell what the object is. A metal detector works this way.

Another archaeologist sifts the soil with a screen. Tiny pieces of soil fall through the holes, but bigger pieces stay on top. The archaeologists look for any charcoal or bits of artifacts that may show them people were once there. Then they walk a little farther and sample the soil again.

Each day, at the end of their fieldwork, the researchers record their discoveries and mark the positions of those discoveries on a map. This information will help archaeologists decide if they should excavate part of the field and where the exact excavation site should be.

How OLD is It?

WOW, LOOK AT THOSE BONES! HOW OLD ARE THEY?

Archaeologists look for artifacts that can be dated. Bones, wood, and especially charcoal can be radiocarbon dated.

How do archaeologists know how old something is? One way is by finding out how much radiocarbon the object contains. Objects that were alive or were made from living things during the past 50,000 years can be dated using this process.

Radiocarbon is found in all organisms, including people, animals, and plants. It is a radioactive form of carbon. Radioactive atoms break down into other substances over time. Human beings and other animals take in new radiocarbon atoms all their lives, chiefly from the plants they eat. Plants absorb radiocarbon from the carbon dioxide in the air.

44

After an organism dies, it can no longer take in radiocarbon. The amount of radiocarbon in the organism's tissues then decreases at a slow, steady rate. The radiocarbon level in the remains of an organism tells scientists when that organism died.

Take an animal bone, for example. Scientists know that half of its radiocarbon will have decayed 5,730 years after the animal it belonged to stopped taking in radiocarbon.

Plants and animals take in radiocarbon while they are alive.

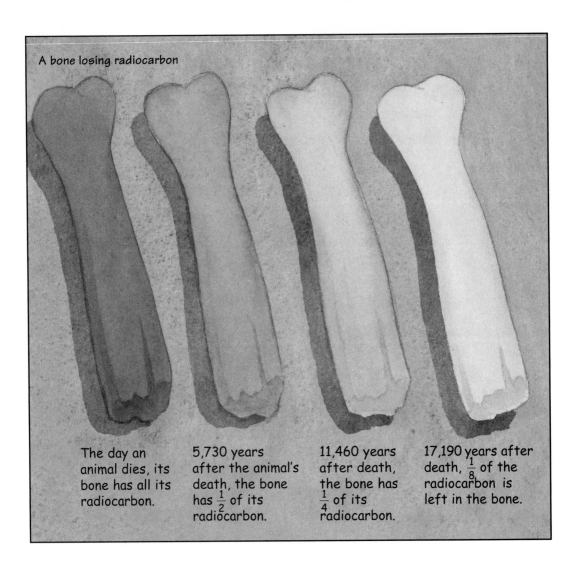

A bone losing radiocarbon

The day an animal dies, its bone has all its radiocarbon.

5,730 years after the animal's death, the bone has $\frac{1}{2}$ of its radiocarbon.

11,460 years after death, the bone has $\frac{1}{4}$ of its radiocarbon.

17,190 years after death, $\frac{1}{8}$ of the radiocarbon is left in the bone.

After another 5,730 years, only one-fourth of the bone's original radiocarbon will remain. After another 5,730 years—or 17,190 years after the animal died—only one-eighth of its radiocarbon will remain. In other words, every 5,730 years, half of the bone's remaining radiocarbon decays. That is why we call 5,730 the half-life of radiocarbon atoms.

If archaeologists can positively date a bone or other organic artifact taken from a site, they may use that information to date other artifacts found near the bone.

But archaeologists have other dating methods, too. Stratigraphy (struh TIHG ruh fee) uses the strata—layers of material—at a site to date something. Usually, artifacts found in the top strata are the youngest. The farther down an artifact is found, the older that item is likely to be.

Strata are the layers of material at a site.

Archaeologists sometimes date artifacts, such as tools and pottery, by comparing them to similar objects that have already been dated. For example, they examine objects to see if they are made of the same materials, have the same shape, or are decorated in the same style.

Tamika's JOURNAL

Dr. McShane invited our class to help with his excavation of a mysterious building in a small ghost town not far from the museum. The town burned to the ground about twelve years ago, and all records were lost. Dr. McShane's team has identified every building except one.

JUNIOR ARCHAEOLOGY TEACHERS:
Dr. Banks and Dr. Carter McShane

AUTHOR:
Tamika

DIG CREW:
Clare, Jamal, Rajiv, Teresa, Mike, Lin, and Tamika

SITE:
The building is 20 miles (32 kilometers) from the Museum of Natural History. Its remains consisted of only a large concrete slab and a metal shaft about 12 feet (3.6 meters) tall.

Dr. McShane suspected that the shaft was a vent from a furnace that took heat to what was the second floor of this building. He called this guess his hypothesis.

WHAT WE DID:
We watched as Dr. McShane cut away one side of the shaft. We were surprised to find that the shaft was packed with pieces of colored paper and chunks of sticky material.

CONCLUSION 1:
The shaft was not used to supply heat to the second floor when the building was in use.

WHAT WE FOUND:

Dr. McShane used an instant camera to photograph the profile of the shaft—the layers showing changes over time. Wearing plastic gloves, we took turns pulling pieces of paper and dried-up material out of the shaft. We started at the top layer, which contained the most recent artifacts. Some of the artifacts appeared dirty and felt spongy—very gross.

Some of us arranged the artifacts in rows that matched the photos. The four main types of artifacts included:

1. Pages of comic books

2. Pieces of candy and candy wrappers

3. Pieces of chewing gum—some chewed and some in their wrapper

4. Crumpled-up school papers, usually with a grade of "D" or "F"

We tried to identify the characters in the comic books as well as the kinds of candy and gum we found. We then took turns using a laptop computer to look up the ages of these artifacts on the Internet.

CONCLUSION 2:

The top layer of the shaft contained pieces of a Super Time Detective comic book. The story told about the death of the Time Detective's sidekick. We found out that this issue of the comic book came out in 1988. So we concluded that the last artifacts were dropped into the shaft in 1988 or later.

CONCLUSION 3:

The bottom layer had no comic books and not many kinds of candy either. We found a couple of Yum and Juicy candies mixed in with chunks of Nutty Butter Bars. From our research, we learned that the first Yum and Juicy candy was made in 1893, but there were no Nutty Butter Bars made until 1916. So the bottom layer is probably not older than 1916.

CONCLUSION 4:

Dr. McShane asked us to review the artifacts and information we gathered and then to make a hypothesis of how the building was used. Clare, Mike, Lin, and Teresa thought the building was a candy store. Jamal and Rajiv thought it was a drugstore that sold candy. My hypothesis was that the building was a school because of the school papers we found.

Dr. McShane and Dr. Banks agreed with me! In the end, we all concluded that the vent was originally under a school desk. We believe that the students who sat at that desk used the vent of the air shaft as a wastebasket to get rid of comic books they should not have been reading in class. (Maybe they were the students who received the bad grades!) They also used the vent to throw away candy they should not have been eating in school.

←Teacher

BAD Grade!→

Candy Wrapper

Vent →

A CITY'S RED LAYER

Reminders of the past are not found only in faraway places. Clues to a violent event in London's history lie right beneath that city's streets! Two amazing archaeological sites found recently reveal information about London's early history, when it was part of the Roman Empire. At both sites, archaeologists found evidence of a bloody battle that destroyed the city only about ten years after it was founded.

The first site lies beneath a new office building in central London. The archaeological crew worked for nearly two years, as subway trains rumbled nearby and construction for the new building went on above them. But for the first time, they were able to learn who lived in a particular area of early Londinium—London's name during Roman times.

They discovered that this area was a business district where shopkeepers and craftworkers lived and worked. The crew found the stumps of wooden posts that once formed the frames or walls of these buildings. The structures had wooden fronts or frames with walls made of dried mud and sticks. The crew found pottery from France, spices, and many other artifacts. Behind the shops, they found stone buildings. This is where the owners and their families and employees lived.

The second site is in Southwark, south of the Thames River. Archaeologists found more shops here during the construction of a new subway line. But they had not known that this area was also destroyed during that great attack on early Londinium.

Both sites lay beneath London's so-called red layer. This layer, which lies about 13 feet (4 meters) underground, is made up of ashes from buildings that burned during the attack on the city. It also contains clay with particles of iron that turned red from the fire's terrible heat. This layer is unmistakable evidence of Queen Boadicea's (boh ad ih SEE uhs) assault on the city in A.D. 60. Angry at the Romans' harsh treatment of her people—the native Britons— the queen and her troops swooped down on Roman settlements, including Londinium. They killed thousands of the city's inhabitants and then burned the city to the ground.

DIG EVEN DEEPER...

DISCOVER YOUR TOWN'S PAST

Look in your community for buildings that have cornerstones. The date on a cornerstone tells you when a building officially began. Find out which building is the oldest. Look in old newspapers at the library or the historical society or talk with longtime residents. Find out what was happening in your community at that time.

This pottery oil lamp was used in London in the first century. The wick burned in the big toe.

53

DIG EVEN DEEPER...
SCRAMBLED FACTS

Archaeologists often find broken parts of various artifacts mixed together. Test your archaeological skills with a friend.

1. Collect several large pictures of flowerpots, plates, vases, or similar colorful items.

2. Ask a friend to cut two or more pictures into pieces of different shapes and sizes, about $1\frac{1}{2}$ inches to 2 inches (4 to 5 centimeters) each. Then put the pieces into a bag and shake them up.

3. Pull out one piece and try to guess what it is part of.

4. Now pour out the other pieces. How long does it take you to put each artifact together?

5. Archaeologists rarely find all the pieces of an artifact. See how missing pieces make the time detective's job even trickier. Ask your friend to cut up two or more pictures and mix the pieces in a bag. This time, ask your friend to take out some of the pieces before giving you the bag.

6. Put together as much of each artifact as you can. Can you figure out what the artifacts are?

What can you learn from looking at the whole picture instead of just at the bits and pieces?

YOU WILL NEED

- old newspapers and magazines (get permission first)
- scissors
- a paper bag
- a friend or two

54

THINKING OUTSIDE *the* BALKS

EVERY ARTIFACT AND ECOFACT FOUND AT A SITE IS LIKE A PIECE OF A PUZZLE. PUT TOGETHER, THE PIECES MAY REVEAL VALUABLE INFORMATION ABOUT THE WAY OF LIFE AT THE SITE.

TIME DETECTIVES NEED TO THINK OUTSIDE THE BALKS (BAWKS) AND LOOK AT THE CLUES FROM THE ENTIRE SITE. BALKS ARE THE OUTSIDE WALLS OF EACH SMALL SQUARE BEING EXCAVATED.

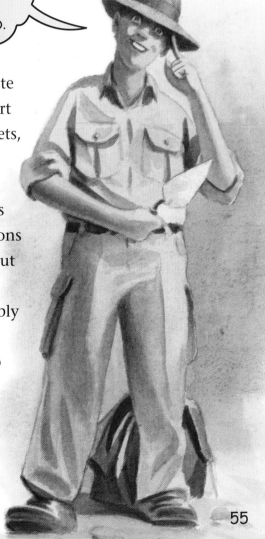

Suppose archaeologists find a site near a deep ditch and they start digging. They soon uncover nets, bunches of small rocks, string, necklaces made of shells, and fish bones. But they don't find the bones of any other animal. What conclusions do you think they may come to about the site?

First, the people there were probably members of a fishing community. The ditch may have been a dried-up river. No other animal bones were found, so the people probably did not raise animals for food or keep them as pets.

On the next few pages, look at the clues—the artifacts and ecofacts—found at four other sites. What do the clues tell you about the food the people ate and the work they did there long ago? Can you tell anything about their housing? If you want a helping hand, look at the junior archaeologist's class notes on page 57. Write down your conclusions. Then read the colored boxes to see what archaeologists have said about such clues.

Clues Group 1:
Burned and butchered bones, charcoal in the middle of a rock firepit, bits of a leather thong and animal skins, baskets, arrowheads, jewelry made of bones, pollen and seeds from local plants.

HUNTERS AND GATHERERS

MOST OF THESE PEOPLE LIVED IN SEMI-PERMANENT HOUSES. THEY PROBABLY FOLLOWED THE ANIMALS THEY HUNTED AND KILLED FOR FOOD. THE CHARCOAL AND THE BUTCHERED ANIMAL BONES SUGGEST THAT THE PEOPLE COOKED THE MEAT OVER OPEN FIRES. THE BASKETS WERE MADE WITH REEDS FROM WILD GRASSES. THE PEOPLE ALSO PROBABLY GATHERED NUTS, BERRIES, AND SEEDS THAT GREW IN THE WILD AND CARRIED THEM IN THE BASKETS. THE PEOPLE MADE CLOTHES AND POUCHES FROM THE HIDES OF THE ANIMALS THEY HUNTED. THESE PEOPLE ARE CALLED HUNTERS AND GATHERERS.

Clues Group 2:
Burned kernels of corn, a weaving shuttle and part of a loom, statues of gods, iron or stone tools for digging or cutting, an assortment of clay bowls.

FARMERS

THESE PEOPLE SEEMED TO HAVE CLEARED FIELDS OF WILD PLANTS IN ORDER TO GROW GRAINS, SUCH AS CORN AND WHEAT. THEY MADE TOOLS OF STONE AND IRON AND OTHER METALS THAT HELPED THEM PLANT AND HARVEST THEIR CROPS. THEY USED BOWLS TO PREPARE THEIR FOOD. PARTS OF CERTAIN PLANTS COULD BE WOVEN INTO CLOTH. THE PEOPLE PRAYED TO RAIN GODS AND SUN GODS FOR GOOD GROWING SEASONS. WE CALL THESE PEOPLE FARMERS.

NOTES FROM JUNIOR ARCHAEOLOGY CLASS

—PREHISTORIC PEOPLE OFTEN USED BOWS AND ARROWS TO HUNT ANIMALS FOR FOOD.

—MANY ANCIENT FARMERS PRAYED TO THE GODS FOR RAIN DURING THE GROWING SEASON.

—JEWELRY WAS MADE OF ITEMS FOUND NEARBY OR OBJECTS TRADED WITH MERCHANTS FROM FAR AWAY. OTHER CLUES ARE NEEDED TO DECIDE MEANING.

—ANIMAL BONES MAY BE EVIDENCE OF WHAT PEOPLE ATE OR THE PETS THEY RAISED. OTHER CLUES ARE NEEDED TO DECIDE MEANING.

Clues Group 3:
Old coins, a large pottery jar, stones with lines on them, jewelry made with precious stones not usually found in this area.

TRADERS

THESE PEOPLE USED OBJECTS, PLANTS, AND ANIMALS FROM FARAWAY PLACES, AS WELL AS PLANTS AND ANIMALS FROM THE SURROUNDING AREA. LARGE JARS HELD GOODS FOR TRADING. THE PEOPLE MAY HAVE USED MONEY. MARKS ON STONES, ROCKS, WOOD, OR THE GROUND WERE PROBABLY USED FOR COUNTING. WE CALL THESE PEOPLE *TRADERS*.

IN THE SPOTLIGHT...

Olga Soffer, born in Yugoslavia, has spent much time looking for clues from the Stone Age. As shown here, she has examined imprints on clay and patterns on carvings. From her studies, she concludes that prehistoric women knew how to process plant fibers and weave them into cloth. A prehistoric woman's wardrobe did not look anything like what Wilma Flintstone wore. Far from always wearing smelly animal hides, she says, they wore clothes of woven fabric—some of it so fine that it looked like linen.

Olga SOFFER
STONE–AGE DETECTIVE

Clues Group 4:
Fence posts; a structure with a firepit; bones from sheep, cows, and horses, with butchering marks on them.

HERDERS

THESE PEOPLE PROBABLY HAD HOUSES THAT THEY LIVED IN MOST OF THE YEAR. THEY ALSO HAD HOUSING FOR THEIR ANIMALS. FROM THE FENCE AND TYPES OF ANIMAL BONES FOUND, IT SEEMS THAT THE ANIMALS GRAZED ON THE LAND. WE CALL THESE PEOPLE *HERDERS*.

NOW TAKE A LOOK AROUND YOUR OWN HOUSE. WHAT EVIDENCE IS THERE OF THE FOODS YOUR FAMILY EATS? WHAT EVIDENCE IS THERE OF THE WORK YOUR FAMILY DOES?

BITS and PIECES

DIG EVEN DEEPER...

WHAT IS IT?

Although metal does not decay, it can rust or corrode. Sometimes this creates a rocklike coating. This photo shows a corroded metal object found at an underwater excavation site. Can you guess what the object is? A picture of the restored artifact is shown on page 63.

Imagine that all the artifacts from all the historical sites ever excavated are piled up in front of you. Which kinds of artifacts would be the most plentiful? You would probably see many stone tools. There would also be many metal objects, such as coins and bracelets. Most definitely there would be a lot of shards—bits and pieces of clay vases, jars, pitchers, and plates. All these types of artifacts are called inorganic. They were never part of a living thing. Stone, metal, and pottery may break, but they do not decay—rot—over the ages.

In that huge pile, though, you would not see many wooden tools, leather belts, or woven baskets. Food scraps and clothing made from linen and cotton would be rare, too. Why? Objects made of organic materials decay at a steady rate. Organic materials are the remains of plants or animals or things made from plants or animals. Bacteria and fungi increase the rate at which these materials decay, eventually leaving just black blotches of soil.

But wait! Many of the organic artifacts that archaeologists have uncovered are thousands of years old. Why didn't they decay? In certain situations, organic materials may be preserved very well.

BACTERIA AND FUNGI MULTIPLY RAPIDLY IN WARM, MOIST AIR. AS A RESULT, ORGANIC MATERIAL ROTS QUICKLY IN HOT, HUMID PLACES. THIS IS WHY ARCHAEOLOGISTS WORKING IN TROPICAL RAIN FORESTS AND JUNGLES USUALLY FIND ONLY INORGANIC RELICS OF THE PAST, SUCH AS POTTERY JARS AND STONE BUILDINGS, AXES, AND ARROWHEADS.

UNDERWATER ARTIFACTS ARE EASILY DESTROYED BY ANIMALS, SALT, AND WATER CURRENTS. BUT SOMETIMES THE ARTIFACTS SETTLE TO THE BOTTOM. THERE, SILT COVERS AND PRESERVES THEM, EVEN FROM BACTERIA AND FUNGI. LEATHER SHOES AND OTHER ORGANIC SHIPWRECKED ARTIFACTS HAVE BEEN FOUND PRESERVED IN THIS WAY.

A SPECIAL TYPE OF WETLAND CALLED A BOG ALSO PRESERVES ORGANIC ARTIFACTS WELL. BACTERIA CANNOT SURVIVE IN A BOG'S ACIDIC SOIL. ARCHAEOLOGISTS HAVE FOUND WELL-PRESERVED WOODEN WHEELS, LEATHER SHOES, AND EVEN HUMAN BODIES IN PEAT BOGS!

FREEZING TEMPERATURES ALSO SLOW DECAY. FOR EXAMPLE, THE 2,000-YEAR-OLD BODY OF A MAN WAS FOUND UNDER SEVERAL FEET OF ICE IN THE ALTAI MOUNTAINS OF CENTRAL ASIA. HIS WOOL HAT AND FUR COAT WERE IN EXCELLENT CONDITION. EVEN MORE ASTONISHING, HIS SKIN WAS SO WELL PRESERVED THAT A TATTOO OF A DEER WAS CLEARLY VISIBLE ON HIS RIGHT SHOULDER.

WHAT THEN IS THE BEST PRESERVATIVE OF ALL? DRY AIR. DRY AIR KEEPS BACTERIA AND FUNGI LEVELS VERY LOW. IT ALSO HELPS KEEP ORGANIC ARTIFACTS INTACT. NEED PROOF? IN ABOUT 1900, ARCHAEOLOGISTS DIGGING IN CHILE'S SUPER-DRY COASTAL DESERT DISCOVERED HUNDREDS OF MUMMIES. THE 7,000-YEAR-OLD BODIES STILL HAD SKIN, TEETH, AND HAIR AND LAY BESIDE WELL-PRESERVED GRASS MATS AND PLANT-FIBER ROPES. DRY CAVES HAVE ALSO PRESERVED SUCH SECRETS OF THE PAST.

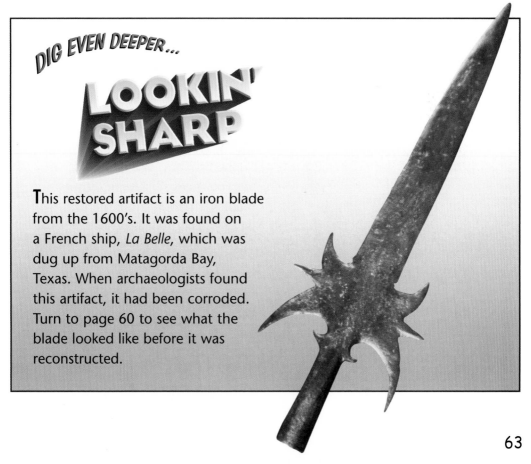

DIG EVEN DEEPER...

LOOKIN' SHARP

This restored artifact is an iron blade from the 1600's. It was found on a French ship, *La Belle*, which was dug up from Matagorda Bay, Texas. When archaeologists found this artifact, it had been corroded. Turn to page 60 to see what the blade looked like before it was reconstructed.

GOING... GOING...
ALMOST GONE

YOU WILL NEED
- several banana slices
- 2 plastic bags
- 1 packet of dry yeast

What's Left?

See for yourself how artifacts made of organic material decay. Find out how cold, dry conditions can slow the process.

1. Place one or two slices of banana in one of the bags.

2. Empty half of the packet of yeast into the bag. Yeast is a kind of fungus.

3. Seal the bag and place it on top of the refrigerator.

4. Repeat steps 1 through 3 with another plastic bag and one or two other banana slices. This time, however, place the bag in the freezer.

Check the bags after one week. How different are the bags of banana slices? The banana slices on top of the refrigerator should show more signs of decay than the ones in the freezer. In the same way, organic material will decay faster in a hot jungle than on a cold mountainside.

Another Way to Go

This experiment shows the effect that acid—in this case, vinegar—has on the rate of decay of an organic material.

YOU WILL NEED
- 2 drinking glasses
- 1 bouillon cube
- 1 cup hot water
- 1 teaspoon white
- vinegar
- masking tape (or other label)
- a permanent marker

1. Ask an adult to help you dissolve the bouillon cube in the hot water. Then pour equal amounts of the broth into the two glasses.

2. Add the vinegar to one of the glasses.

3. Write "vinegar" on a piece of masking tape and stick it on the glass containing vinegar. Label the other glass "no vinegar."

4. Place the glasses in a warm place for two days.

What do you see? The liquid in the "no vinegar" glass should be cloudy. This shows that bacteria are present. The liquid in the glass labeled "vinegar" should be clear. It is clear because the acid stopped the growth of bacteria. Peat bogs are acidic places that slow the decay of most organic materials.

No Bones About It

Acid can help preserve some things, but it destroys others. What do you think it does to bones? Do this simple activity to find out.

1. Pour vinegar into the jar.

2. Place the bone or shells in the vinegar.

3. Screw the lid on tightly.

YOU WILL NEED
- a jar and lid
- vinegar
- a dry chicken bone (or eggshells)

Check the contents daily for a week. What happens? At first, the ends of the bone should become soft. Eventually, the bone should bend like rubber. After a week, the acid will eat holes in the shells. Although acidic soil preserves most organic materials, it dissolves bones and shells. As a result, some bodies found in peat bogs have well-preserved hair and organs but spongy bones.

DIGGING *for* CAMELOT

According to legend, a ruler named King Arthur once lived in an English castle called Camelot. Arthur and his army of Britons supposedly defeated a large force of Saxons. The Saxons were one of three Germanic tribes, along with the Angles and Jutes, who invaded England in the late 400's or early 500's. A real King Arthur probably existed, but historians know almost nothing about him.

FEATURED ATTRACTION...

Almost no words in modern English come from the language spoken by the ancient Britons. But about thirty percent of the words English speakers use today come from the language of the Germanic invaders who overran England in the A.D. 400's and 500's. Their language is now known as Old English or Anglo-Saxon. The words include *book, child, friend, ghost, hip,* and *shoe.*

For hundreds of years, people in southwestern England have insisted that a famous hilltop fortress called Cadbury Castle was actually Camelot. From the top of this hill, you can see for miles around. It is an ideal place for defending an army against attackers.

In the mid-1950's, an archaeologist found shards of pottery in a freshly plowed field near Cadbury Castle. The shards were identified as a kind of pottery that was made in the late 400's and early 500's. This find inspired Professor Leslie Alcock and his team of archaeologists to search the area for Camelot. They began working in 1966.

Aerial photographs offered few clues about where to start digging on the 18-acre (7-hectare) area. So the crew used other instruments to survey what was underground. Based on these findings, the professor chose an excavation site

DIG EVEN DEEPER...

TO DIG OR NOT TO DIG

Archaeology is full of questions and puzzles. And sometimes a discovery can stir up controversy and tough decisions. What if you found ancient jewels on your land, but they originally came from people who lived far away in another country. Who should have the right to study and house the precious relics?

Imagine an archaeologist finds a burial site. Suppose that one of your ancient ancestors is buried there. How would you and your family feel about the site being dug? Now suppose your religion says that the graves of ancestors must not be disturbed, because the spirit of the dead person might then haunt your family. How would you and your family feel? What if the artifacts at that site were very important—they would teach archaeologists and other people around the world about how people at that site lived very long ago? Are the religious beliefs of one group of people more important than learning about the past?

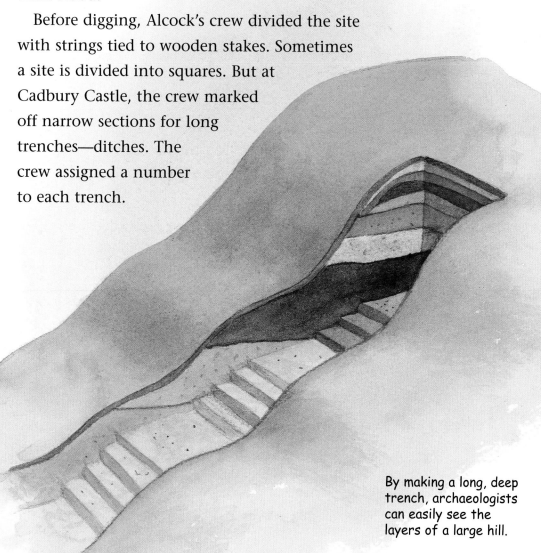

where he believed the inner walls of the fort once stood.

Before digging, Alcock's crew divided the site with strings tied to wooden stakes. Sometimes a site is divided into squares. But at Cadbury Castle, the crew marked off narrow sections for long trenches—ditches. The crew assigned a number to each trench.

By making a long, deep trench, archaeologists can easily see the layers of a large hill.

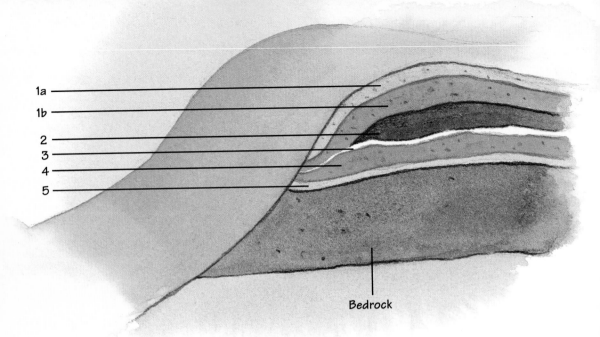

1a
1b
2
3
4
5

Bedrock

Archaeologists found artifacts in the top six layers of soil at Cadbury. They numbered the layers as shown above. When layers have only minor changes in color or texture, as they did at Cadbury, archaeologists give them the same number but different letters.

Earth-moving machines were used to dig the first deep trench. From inside the trench, the professor could clearly see the site's profile. The strata represented six different periods in the history of Cadbury Castle. Each layer was given a number. The first trench served as a guide to excavating the other trenches at the site.

For the second trench, the crew dug with picks and shovels until they came to the first layer that contained archaeological features. Features include buildings, walls, and other structures made by people that cannot be moved easily. The Cadbury features included stones from a wall built during the late 900's. According to historical records, the wall was part of a fort that the English king Ethelred II had raised to fight off Viking raiders. The fort was abandoned in 1017, the year after Ethelred died.

Next, the crew began using trowels to uncover artifacts from the Ethelred period.

These were placed in bags and labeled with the numbers of the field, trench, and layer where they were found. Then the artifacts were set aside for later study.

The stones and other features that could not be bagged and saved had to be cleared away to reach the next layer. So the workers drew a floor plan—a picture of the excavated area—before continuing to dig.

Over the next few years, Professor Alcock and his team excavated several more trenches. In the layer under King Ethelred's fort, they found signs of a great hall surrounded by a walled-in area big enough to house an army! Important artifacts from this layer included a coin, a brooch, and shards of painted pottery from the late 400's or early 500's—when King Arthur supposedly ruled England.

The dig at Cadbury Castle showed that the fort's inhabitants were wealthy enough to afford expensive pottery. And they were numerous and strong enough to have stopped a Saxon invasion. The discoveries at Cadbury Castle did not prove that Arthur existed. But they showed that the fortress was strongly fortified around the time that the legendary Arthur supposedly lived.

FEATURED ATTRACTION...

The earliest layers at Cadbury Castle showed that the ancient Britons had built a village that flourished for hundreds of years. Sometime before A.D. 100, Roman invaders attacked the village and drove off the survivors. The hill remained mostly unoccupied until after the Romans left England in the early 400's.

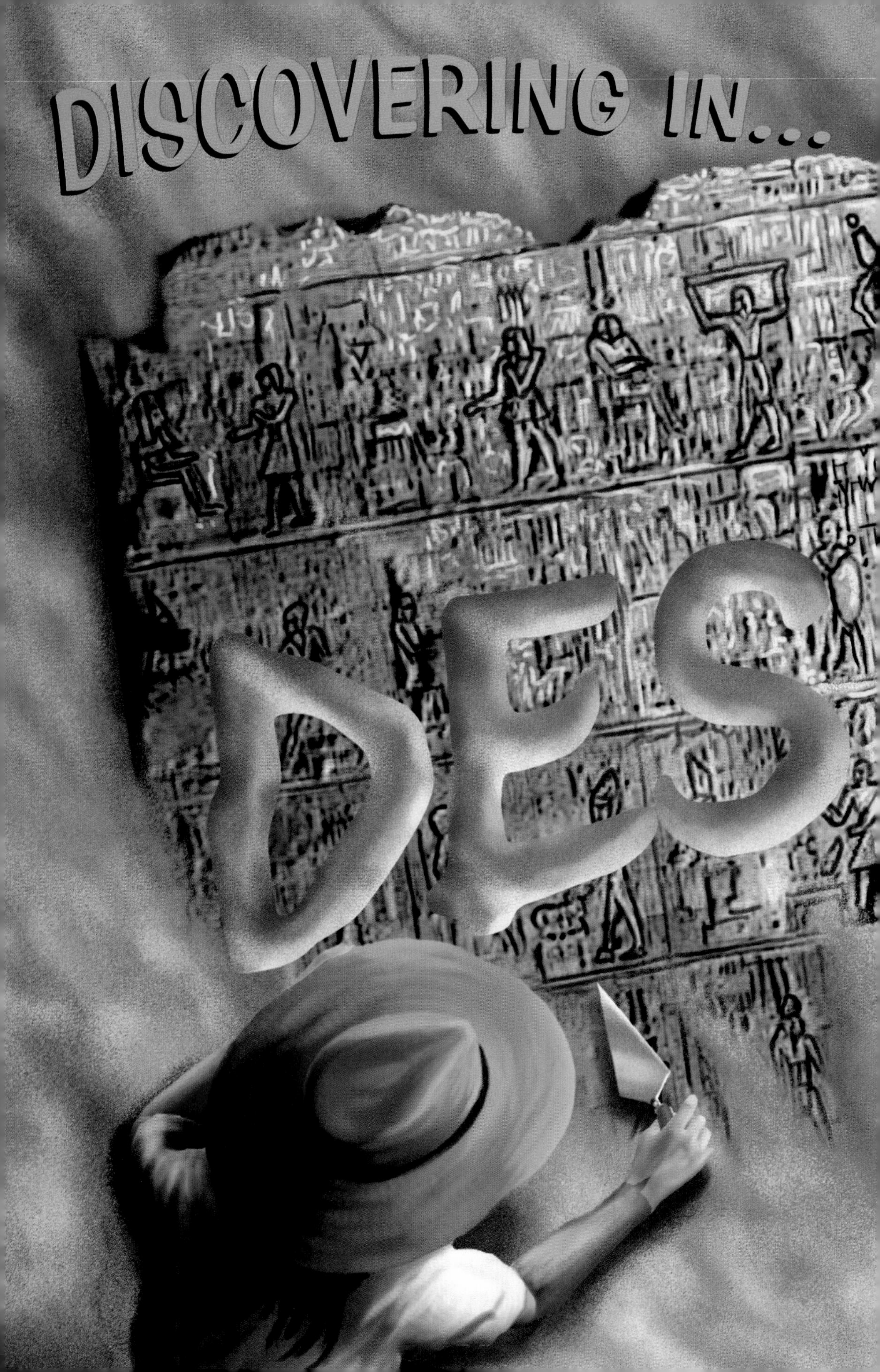
DISCOVERING IN...
DES

King Tut UNWRAPPED!

AZYEK (UH ZAY EHK)! THAT'S HOW EGYPTIANS SAY "HELLO." MY NAME IS HORUS, MEANING FALCON, AND I AM GOING TO TELL YOU ABOUT THE MUMMY OF KING TUT. KING TUT IS THE MOST FAMOUS EGYPTIAN PHARAOH.

BUT TUTANKHAMEN—THAT WAS HIS REAL NAME—DID NOT BECOME FAMOUS FOR ANYTHING HE DID.

MOST PEOPLE KNOW ABOUT HIM TODAY BECAUSE OF THE INCREDIBLE TREASURES FOUND IN HIS TOMB.

TUTANKHAMEN RULED AS EGYPT'S PHARAOH, OR KING, FOR NEARLY TEN YEARS. HE WAS ONLY ABOUT 18 YEARS OLD WHEN HE DIED SUDDENLY IN 1339 B.C., MORE THAN 3,300 YEARS AGO.

LIKE THE PEOPLE OF MANY OTHER CULTURES, THE ANCIENT EGYPTIANS BELIEVED IN A LIFE AFTER DEATH. THEY BELIEVED THAT WHEN A PERSON DIED, SPIRITS CALLED THE BA AND KA LEFT THE BODY. ONLY WHEN THESE SPIRITS RETURNED TO THE BODY COULD IT LIVE IN THE AFTERLIFE. BUT THE BODY HAD TO BE PRESERVED AND MADE PURE BEFORE IT WOULD BE READY TO RECEIVE THE SPIRITS.

early 5,000 years ago, the ancient
Egyptians began to mummify
(MUHM uh fy) dead bodies to
prevent them from decaying. They
treated the dead bodies with chemicals.
Then the corpses were dried. This
process is called embalming, and the
Egyptians became very good at it.

ANCIENT EGYPTIANS
BELIEVED THAT THE
GOD ANUBIS, WHO
OFTEN APPEARED IN
THE FORM OF A DOG,
OVERSAW THE
PREPARATION OF
MUMMIES FOR BURIAL.

The embalming process that was used
for wealthy people and royalty, like King
Tut, took seventy days. The process used for
poorer people was not as complicated. In
Tut's case, the embalmers first removed his
brain and other organs, except his heart.
They embalmed his liver, lungs, stomach,
and intestines, placed them in separate jars,
and buried them in his tomb.

The embalmers left Tut's heart inside his
dead body because they believed that the

heart was the center of intelligence. Clearly, Tut would need his heart in the afterlife. They threw the brain away because they thought it was not important.

Next, the embalmers stuffed pieces of linen (cloth made of a plant fiber) into Tut's body to fill it out and make it appear more lifelike. The embalmers then dried the body by covering it with a powdered mineral called natron (NAY trahn) for forty days. Natron also slowed the growth of bacteria, which causes decay.

When Tut's body was dried, the embalmers washed it with wine and spices. Then they coated it with tree resin and special oils to preserve it and help prevent the skin from cracking. Tut's mummy, as his embalmed body was called, was then wrapped tightly and carefully in strips of linen. It could take fifteen days to wrap a mummy!

The embalming process in ancient Egypt could take seventy days. The first panel below shows organs being removed, embalmed, and placed in jars. In the second panel, the body is washed in wine and spices and coated in special oils. In the third panel, embalmers wrap the body tightly and carefully in strips of linen.

A beautifully decorated, solid-gold mask covered Tut's head and shoulders. And gold caps covered his toes! Tut's mummy was placed into a solid-gold coffin, and then into a gold-plated wooden coffin, then into another gold-plated wooden coffin. The mummy and its three coffins went into one last coffin made of stone and called a sarcophagus (sahr KAHF uh guhs). *Sarcophagus* is a Greek word meaning "flesh-eating." Finally, everything was placed into a large tomb.

Most mummies did not get such royal treatment, though. The masks of ordinary people were usually carved out of wood or made of linen or a type of plant called papyrus (puh PY ruhs), and held together by glue. The person's facial features were painted on the mask. A thin layer of gold often covered the masks of wealthier people. Coffins could be simple wooden boxes or cases shaped like a body and painted with colorful designs and figures.

The ancient Egyptians also buried their dead with food, clothing, money, and other things they thought the dead person would need in the afterlife.

King Tut's gold death mask

Tut's tomb contained more than 5,000 artifacts, including jewelry, clothing, thrones, beds, chariots, swords, toys, games, trumpets, and models of ships. He also had 413 ushabtis (yoo SHAB teez), small statues that were said to do the hard work people were expected to do in the afterlife.

A British archaeologist named Howard Carter discovered Tut's tomb in the Valley of the Kings, a cemetery where Egypt's kings and queens had been buried for hundreds of years. Most archaeologists of that time believed that Tut's tomb had already been robbed of all its treasures. But Carter kept digging anyway. He spent nearly six years searching for the tomb. Then, in 1922, during his last season in the valley, he found it—by accident.

A worker on the dig was kicking rocks aside to make a place for his water jug when he stubbed his foot on something solid underneath the sand. It was the top step of a buried staircase. At the bottom of that staircase, Carter found the entrance to the tomb of Tutankhamen.

After spending several days clearing away stone and rubble, Carter peered through a peephole he had made in a door. On the other side of the door, he saw the glittering of gold everywhere.

FEATURED ATTRACTION...

Was there a mummy's curse? Lord Carnarvon, the person who provided the money for the search for Tut's tomb, died of pneumonia (noo MOHN yuh) less than two months after Tut's mummy was found. His death sparked reports that Tutankhamen had placed a curse on anyone who disturbed his tomb. But a study of the people who worked on the excavation revealed that most lived long after the discovery of Tut's mummy.

TUT'S MUMMY STILL LIES IN ITS DISCOVERED TOMB. BUT THE TREASURES, SOME OF WHICH ARE SHOWN ABOVE IN THE TOMB, ARE NOW ON EXHIBIT IN THE *CAIRO MUSEUM* IN EGYPT. ARCHAEOLOGISTS CONTINUE TO STUDY THE ARTIFACTS TO LEARN MORE ABOUT THE LIFE OF THIS FAMOUS BOY-KING AND HIS KINGDOM.

The discovery of Tut's tomb created an international sensation. Archaeologists have found dozens of tombs in the Valley of the Kings, but Tut's tomb is the only one that had remained almost completely undisturbed by grave robbers.

No one knows for sure why Tut died at such a young age. But in 1996, one scientist offered new evidence that Tut may have been murdered! He studied X rays of Tut's head made in 1968. The X rays showed a white line at the base of his skull. This line could be a sign that a blood clot had formed there because someone had delivered a deadly blow to his head.

The scientist suggested that the murderer may have been Ay, Tut's chief adviser. After Tut's death, Ay married Tut's widow and became pharaoh (FAIR oh).

Only a few people agree with this theory though. Some scientists think Tut could have died from a fall or a hunting accident. An inscription on the handle of a fan found in Tut's tomb suggests that the pharaoh often hunted. Other scientists have argued that the people who unwrapped Tut's mummy in the mid-1920's may have cracked his skull themselves while examining it.

IN THE SPOTLIGHT...
Howard CARTER
EXCAVATOR of TUTANKHAMEN

Howard Carter, shown here exiting Tut's tomb, learned about archaeology first by drawing, not by digging. He worked as the illustrator on many excavations before leading the Tutankhamen dig. At a site, an illustrator may draw what an artifact looks like or exactly where it was found and what was found with it. Illustrators may also regularly record the top or side views of part of a site. These drawings can be examined long after the layers have been dug through.

What's So GREAT ABOUT GOLD?

GOLDIE, YOU KEEP SHOWING UP IN TOMB AFTER ANCIENT TOMB—IT SEEMS EVERYONE WANTED TO TAKE A LITTLE OF YOU INTO ETERNITY WITH THEM. WHAT IS THE SECRET OF YOUR LONG-LASTING POPULARITY?

WELL, YOU HIT ON ONE REASON WHEN YOU SAID "ETERNITY." I AM ONE OF THE FEW METALS THAT WILL NEVER RUST OR CORRODE. I KEEP MY BEAUTIFUL GLOW FOREVER, WHICH BRINGS ME TO ANOTHER REASON I AM SPECIAL. I AM THE ONLY METAL BESIDES COPPER THAT IS COLORED.

The back of Tut's gold-covered throne, below, shows the sun with hands at the ends of its rays. The queen is rubbing oil on the king.

MY COLOR IS SO LOVELY THAT THE ANCIENT EGYPTIANS THOUGHT MY SHINING BEAUTY STOOD FOR THEIR SUN GOD.

VALLEY of the GOLDEN MUMMIES

One of the most amazing things about the discovery of a 2,000-year-old cemetery in the Bahariyah (bah hah REE yah) Oasis in Egypt was that no one was looking for it. No one even knew it existed. It had been completely buried by sand.

ALTHOUGH ARCHAEOLOGISTS HAVE BEEN DIGGING IN EGYPT FOR ABOUT 200 YEARS, THEY ARE STILL MAKING EXCITING DISCOVERIES! HERE AT BAHARIYAH OASIS IN CENTRAL EGYPT, ARCHAEOLOGISTS HAVE FOUND A 2,000-YEAR-OLD CEMETERY.

YES, AND IT MIGHT CONTAIN AS MANY AS 10,000 MUMMIES.

In 1996, a donkey belonging to a guard at the nearby Temple of Alexander the Great stumbled into a hole in the sand a mile from the temple. When the guard peered into the hole, he saw something shining! He reported the discovery to Egyptian archaeologists right away. If archaeologists have known about this site since 1996, why have they excavated only a few hundred mummies? What is taking them so long?

At first, archaeologists' work in this ancient cemetery was top secret to help guard against looters.

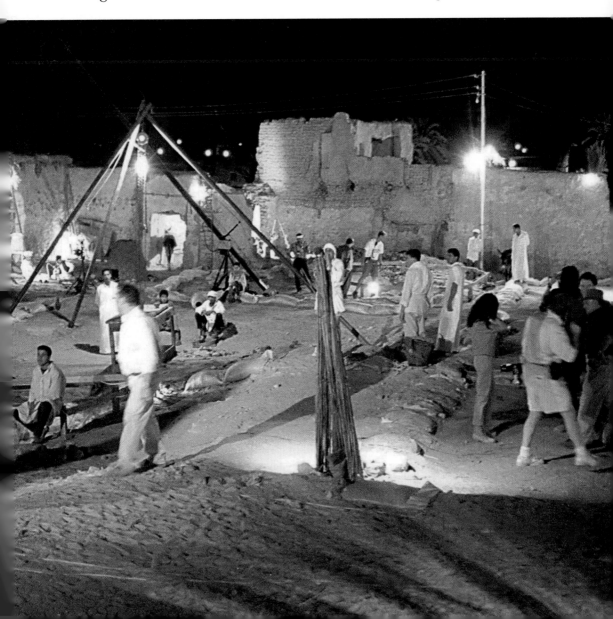

They did not have the workers or the money to start digging right away. So they made a quick survey of the site, and then covered everything up again. They wanted to hide it from thieves and protect it from exposure to sand and weather. Finally, in 1999, they had enough money to begin exploring the site.

These archaeologists really had to be patient. But it was worth the wait. On their very first day of work, after digging only several feet into the sand, they found a lot of mummies. One of them had an especially beautiful gilded mask.

It was not a pharaoh's mummy, though. It turned out that none of the tombs in this cemetery belonged to royalty. Most of the people buried here came from families that grew rich by trading wine. Archaeologists think most of the mummies were buried here in the first 200 years after Christ's birth, when the Roman Empire ruled Egypt. For 300 years before that, Greece had controlled Egypt. The hairstyles and clothing painted on the mummies' masks show that Roman and Greek customs were mixed with those of Egypt during that time.

The most spectacular of these mummies have masks made of plaster covered with a thin layer of gold. Some also have gilded plates over their chests. Many are in wonderful condition. And because grave robbers never found these tombs, everything that was buried with them is still there.

Most of the mummies have been left where they were found, but a few of the best-preserved

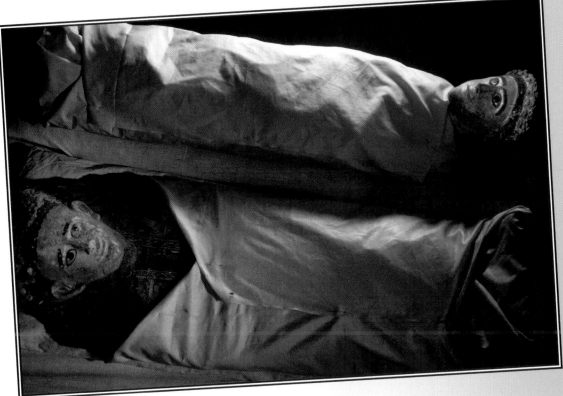

ones are on display in the Bahariyah Museum, where the public can take a look at them.

Two mummies were found lying side by side and are probably a husband and wife. His mask and chest plate are decorated with religious figures. Her head was turned in his direction, indicating that the husband died first.

Two other mummies are of children. Archaeologists think they were brother and sister because they were found together. The boy was probably about 5 years old. His gilded mask with its painted eyes and features are so real—he almost seems alive!

Did archaeologists find treasures in these tombs? It depends on what you mean by "treasures." They have not found any solid-gold artifacts. But they have discovered all sorts of objects.

The people buried in the cemetery may have thought some of these items would be useful in the afterlife. Or some may have been intended as gifts to the gods. For example, archaeologists have unearthed small statues of various gods. They have found many pieces of jewelry— necklaces, bracelets, and anklets— made of copper, glass, ivory, and semiprecious stones. They have also discovered many pottery pieces used for storing, cooking, or serving food. There were some bronze Greek and Roman coins too. And in the children's tombs, they found toys—carved animals for the children to play with in the afterlife!

Archaeologists will be able to learn more about these people and their way of life by further studying their mummies and the artifacts buried with them. And so many mummies were buried in the Valley of the Golden Mummies, excavation and learning will continue at the site for years to come!

GUARDING *the* GRAVES

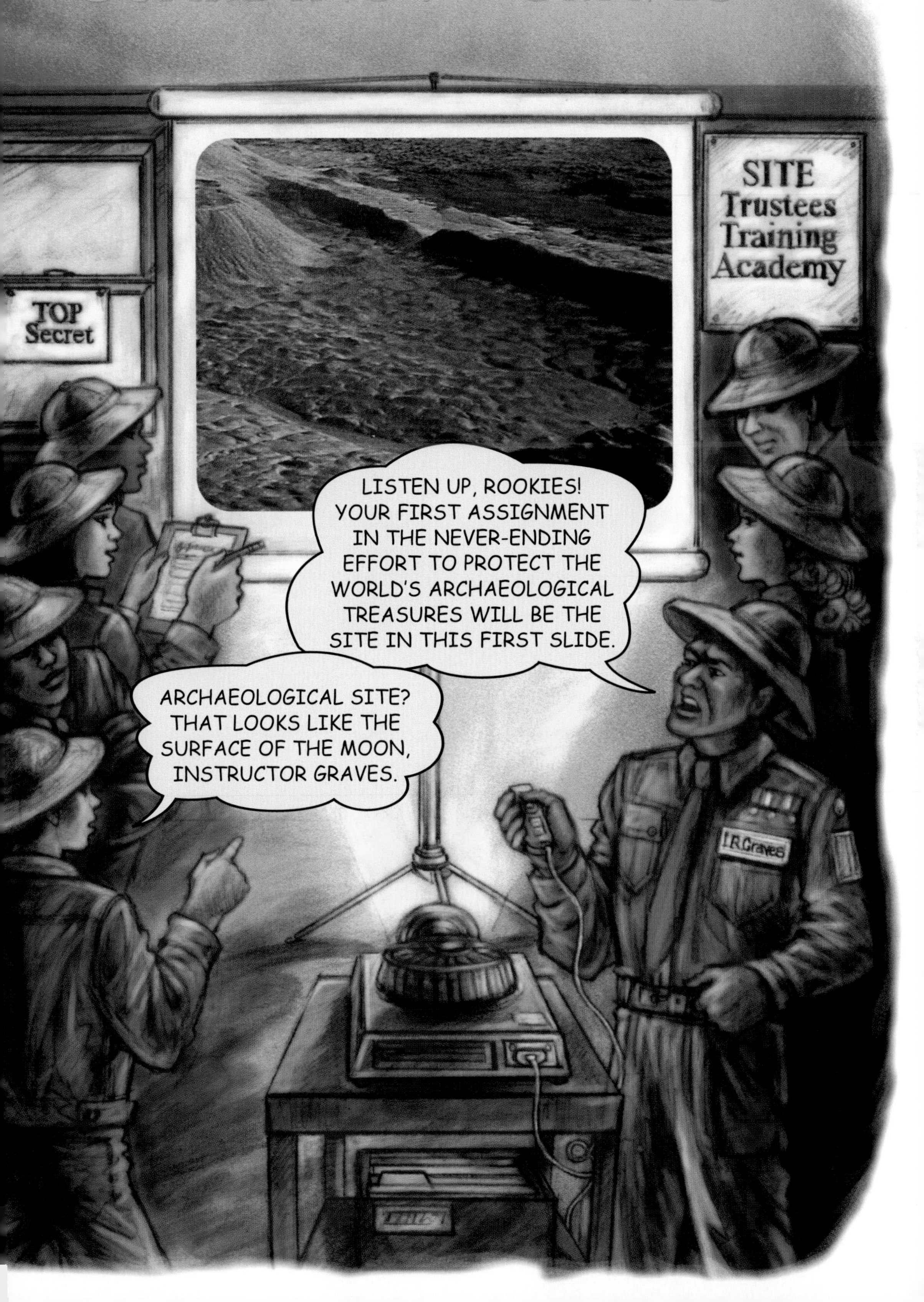

No, it is not—instructor Graves continued with his class. It is a desert on the northern coast of Peru, near the city of Sipán. Those holes were dug by looters. Looters have been uncovering and robbing ancient graves here for more than 450 years—and some are probably doing that at this very minute!

You are probably wondering, what do they think they can find in such an empty place?

They are looking for fantastic artifacts of the people of the Moche (MOH chay) culture. The Moche lived here between A.D. 100 and A.D. 800. They made especially beautiful pottery, as well as many objects of gold, silver, and copper.

Some of the earliest looters were the conquistadors (kahn KEES tuh dawrz). They were the Spaniards who invaded this region in the 1500's and 1600's. In 1938, a very large theft occurred too. A man bulldozed a pyramid and reportedly took fifteen large bags of gold items. Today, many of the looters are poor local people. They sell the artifacts for next to nothing to people who resell them to collectors and other people who want to own them.

So, after hundreds of years of looting, is anything left?

Yes! In 1987, looters found the tomb of a Moche ruler that contained wonderful pottery and gold. When news of their fabulous discovery spread, a team of archaeologists and police came

The Moche were famous for their detailed pottery. The face of a Moche warrior is shown on this stirrup jar. It is called a stirrup jar because the handle looks like a stirrup.

to stop the looting. The archaeologists went on to find nine more tombs of Moche rulers, each one containing more than 500 artifacts of gold, silver, copper, and other precious materials!

Did that excavation uncover all the treasures left in the tombs?

Not quite. Between 1997 and 1999, archaeologists found three more Moche tombs just 40 miles (64 kilometers) south of Sipán. They were all found hidden along the side of a 105-foot- (31-meter-) tall brick-and-mud pyramid. Conquistadors had dug a huge hole in the middle of the pyramid when they were searching for riches. Later, grave robbers had also looked there. But the best part of the story is that they had all missed the tombs, which had not even been touched when the archaeologists excavated them!

Unfortunately, stolen artifacts are not recovered often. And few of the thieves are ever caught. But one important success story is what I call the *flap over the backflap*.

Take a look at the screen. This splendid artifact, made of gold, copper, and silver, is called a backflap. A Moche warrior wore it to protect his rump in combat. It looks similar to his headdress. This backflap was stolen from a tomb in 1987. It was smuggled out of Peru and finally showed up ten years later and thousands of miles away in Pennsylvania. Two men wanted to sell it for $1.6 million.

Unfortunately for the sellers, the "buyers" were law-enforcement agents working undercover. The backflap was sent to the Museum of the Nation in Lima, Peru. And the men who tried to sell it were put in prison.

It is certainly wonderful to have the backflap back in Peru. But it had lost most of its value as an archaeological artifact. Archaeologists can learn a great deal about a culture by studying artifacts in their context—where they were originally placed and how they were grouped together. The backflap's context is gone forever though. In the case of the Moche, this lost information is even more tragic. Sadly, the Moche left no written language for us to decode and help us learn about their culture.

93

BURIED

UNDER BROADWAY

Archaeologists have found many burial grounds in remote deserts, but they have also uncovered one in the middle of bustling New York City. In 1991, construction workers digging the foundation for a new building on Broadway—one of New York's most famous streets—uncovered human bones! The bones were from a 300-year-old graveyard.

Historical records say that during the late 1600's and 1700's, many of New York City's black residents buried their dead in this large graveyard. Most of the people buried there were Africans who had been kidnapped from their homeland and sold as slaves. Some were descendants of those Africans. Originally, the graveyard lay just outside the city's boundaries.

But by the 1790's, the city had expanded to the burial ground. The city then purchased the land and built houses and a street there.

Archaeologists have excavated more than 400 graves in what is now known as the African Burial Ground. The graves contained artifacts, such as beads, pottery, quartz crystal, coins, rings, cuff links, and brightly colored snail shells called cowrie (KAHW ree) shells. Copper pins were used to fasten the clothes that wrapped the dead. The findings have revealed an amazing amount of information about how black New Yorkers lived 300 years ago.

Some of the artifacts suggested that the dead or their ancestors had come from western and central Africa. Several skulls had their teeth filed in a style that was common in certain areas of western and central Africa. More than 100 glass beads and cowrie shells draped the waist of one woman's skeleton. This suggested that she was a member of the region's cultures that traditionally buried beads with the dead.

The skeletons also showed how harsh life was for enslaved Africans in old New York. The bones of many skeletons showed signs of weakness and illness caused by not having enough healthful foods. They also indicated that these people had spent most of their lives doing very hard physical work.

No gold artifacts were found in the African Burial Ground. But to archaeologists, the bones and simple objects found there are as valuable as all the treasures of King Tut.

DIG EVEN DEEPER...
GRAVE FINDER

Take a pencil and paper and visit a cemetery. Find the oldest or most prominent grave and write down the name and dates that appear on it. Does the grave tell you anything else about the person? Are there other gravestones around it marked with the same last name? Go to the library and see if you can find out more about that person or family in local newspapers of the time.

HERE LIES
DOCTOR
JOHN SPARROW
BORN   DIED
JULY 17   JUNE 13
1656   1706

Enameled
cuff links

CLOTHES Make the MUMMY

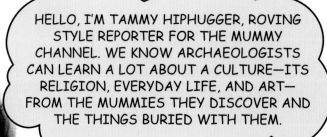

HELLO, I'M TAMMY HIPHUGGER, ROVING STYLE REPORTER FOR THE MUMMY CHANNEL. WE KNOW ARCHAEOLOGISTS CAN LEARN A LOT ABOUT A CULTURE—ITS RELIGION, EVERYDAY LIFE, AND ART— FROM THE MUMMIES THEY DISCOVER AND THE THINGS BURIED WITH THEM.

BUT CAN THEY TELL US ANYTHING ABOUT FASHION? TO FIND OUT, I HAVE TRAVELED TO THE MUSEUM IN THE CITY OF ÜRÜMQI, 1,600 MILES WEST OF BEIJING, CHINA. I AM INTERVIEWING PROFESSOR SANDY TOOMBS ABOUT WHAT HAS BEEN UNCOVERED IN THE TAKLIMAKAN DESERT IN THE TARIM BASIN AREA.

"So, Sandy," said Tammy, "can you tell our viewers what the well-dressed resident of this Chinese desert wore 3,000 years ago?"

"If you will step over here," replied Sandy, "I will introduce you to a strikingly dressed couple. We call them Cherchen Woman and Cherchen Man because they were found in a tomb near the city of that name."

"Incredible! That man looks so well preserved!" remarked Tammy.

"It is amazing, isn't it?" said Sandy. "There are several reasons for their remarkable condition. The mummies were coated with an animal protein to preserve them. The extreme dryness of the desert sands also helped prevent the bodies from decaying. And by complete chance, they were buried in tombs dug into naturally occurring salt beds. Although the people performing the burials probably did not know this, the salt acted as a third preservative—like the natron the Egyptians used in their mummification.

"When Cherchen Woman was discovered, she was wearing a long-sleeved gown of deep-red wool. Such a full-length garment might not flatter a short woman, but Cherchen Woman could carry it off because she was over 6 feet (182 centimeters) tall! She also wore white deerskin boots. Cherchen Man was 6 feet 6 inches (198 centimeters) tall!"

Cherchen Man

97

DIG EVEN DEEPER...
MAKE YOUR OWN "MUMMY"

Ask an adult to help you peel a small apple and cut it in half. Put each half in a plastic cup. Mix one-half cup of baking soda and one-half cup of salt in a bowl. Pour this mixture over one apple slice, being sure to cover it completely. Put both cups on a shelf out of direct sunlight. After one week, carefully pour the baking soda and salt out of the cup. Compare the two apple pieces—but do not eat either! Which slice is better preserved?

"Why has the color remained so rich and bold for 3,000 years?" asked Tammy.

"The dryness not only helped keep the textiles (TEHKS tuhlz) from decaying but also preserved their colors," explained Sandy. "Plus, salt can brighten some colors."

"Those are wild socks on Cherchen Man!" exclaimed Tammy.

"They are actually leggings made of wool felt," said Sandy. "He also wore white deerskin boots, but one of them had disappeared by the time he was found. His woolen shirt and pants are an intriguing reddish-brown color that is often found in Cherchen clothing. Mulberry might be a good name for it. The mummy of a baby found in a nearby tomb was wrapped in a cloth of the same color. Its head was covered by a bright royal-blue woolen cap."

Tammy questioned, "Were other colors and patterns popular among the mummies from Cherchen?"

"Oh, yes," answered Sandy. "Archaeologists have excavated only a few of the hundreds of tombs around Cherchen. They have found mummies with garments in vibrant swirls of red and blue on a yellow background, diamond designs, and multicolored zigzags, just to mention a few."

"Did these people like brightly colored textiles more than the people of other ancient cultures did?" asked Tammy.

"Probably not," replied Sandy. "Many cultures buried textiles with their dead, and they were probably very colorful and attractive. But in Cherchen, as in Egypt, the constant dryness has preserved clothing that would have rotted away long ago in a damper climate."

THANK YOU, SANDY, FOR SHARING THESE MARVELOUS CLOTHES WITH US. TUNE IN NEXT WEEK WHEN THE MUMMY CHANNEL CHECKS OUT THE PATTERNS OF MUMMY BALES—THE CLOTH BUNDLES WRAPPED AROUND PERUVIAN MUMMIES.

the MUMMY CHANNEL

FEATURED ATTRACTION...

Who were those tall, well-dressed strangers? Cherchen Man, Cherchen Woman, and many other mummies found throughout China's Tarim Basin puzzle archaeologists. The mummies were tall people, with prominent, narrow noses, red or blonde hair, and mustaches and beards (on just the men!). They were much different physically from the Chinese people of 3,000 years ago. They look like Europeans, but the Chinese have long believed their civilization had no important contact with Europeans that long ago. So, who were these people? Where did they come from? What happened to them? No one knows.

Felines DIVINE

HELLO, MY NAME IS ISIS. I LIVE IN THE EGYPTIAN CITY OF BUBASTIS. THE YEAR IS 450 B.C., AND BELIEVE ME, IT IS A GREAT TIME AND PLACE TO BE A CAT.

The cat is the sacred animal of Bastet, the kind goddess who brings pleasure, good health, and the power of life from the sun to those who worship her. Bastet has the body of a woman and the head of a cat. She is one of the most popular gods in all of Egypt. Bubastis is the center for worship of Bastet and of cats.

In Egypt, we cats are pampered and protected. We are fed bread, milk, and a lot of raw fish. If a house catches on fire, people do not worry about saving their belongings. They rescue the cats. Sometimes people stand in a circle around a burning building to keep cats from running back into it.

A person who kills a cat, on purpose or even by accident, is liable to be executed. The death of a house cat, even from old age or sickness, saddens everyone who lives in the house. To

Talk about a mummy cat-astrophe, the ancient Beni Hasan cat cemetery in Egypt was forgotten until a farmer found it in 1888. It contained about 300,000 cat mummies! No one who understood its archaeological importance learned about the discovery until it was too late. Local children sold a few of the finest mummies to tourists or kept them as toys. But the rest—56,000 pounds (25,400 kilograms) of cat mummies—were sold in England and ground up as fertilizer.

This cat mummy was wrapped and painted more than 2,000 years ago.

show their sorrow, the members of the family shave their eyebrows.

When a cat dies, the cat's spirits—its ka and ba—leave it. To make sure that the ka and ba will be able to return to the cat's body, the grieving owners mummify the corpse.

The process used to mummify a cat is much the same as the process used for people. After the cat's internal organs are removed, the body is packed with soil or sand to give it a natural shape. It is then wrapped in strips of linen that have been treated with natron or resin. The wrapping is sometimes done in a fancy crisscross pattern.

A cat's owner might bury it in a special coffin shaped like the animal. These are usually made of wood or bronze and often have a cat's face painted on them.

Sometimes a cat is buried with its owner. But most people bury their mummified cats at one of the special cat cemeteries in cities like Thebes, Bubastis, and Beni Hasan.

The Egyptians mummify other animals they consider sacred, including bulls, jackals, scarab beetles, fish, crocodiles, and birds, especially falcons and ibises. But the cat is the most revered animal of all.

FEATURED ATTRACTION...

Here is a sacred secret weapon. The ancient Egyptians' belief in the sacredness of animals helped bring about their country's defeat. In 525 B.C., a Persian king named Cambyses decided to conquer Egypt. When the Egyptian and Persian armies met on one of the battlefields, Cambyses released cats, dogs, ibises, and other animals sacred to the Egyptians in front of his army. Worried that a sacred animal would be hurt or killed, the Egyptians retreated. Cambyses soon became Egypt's ruler.

I Am the Mummy Heb-Nefert

I AM THE mummy Heb-Nefert,
black as night,
stretched as tight
as leather on a drum.
My arms are folded
on my hollow chest
where once my live heart beat.
My ears are holes
that hear no sound.
Once I was the daughter of a nomarch,
favored, beautiful.
But all things change.

Handmaidens dressed me every day.
They kept my head so sweetly shaved,
pumiced and polished till it shone.
They painted me with yellow dye,
darkened the lashes of my eyes with kohl,
shadowed my lids with blue,
the color of the evening sky.
My nails were hennaed red as jasper beads,
my flaxen wig was jewel woven.
And on the top
a cone of scented fat
melted to liquid in the summer warmth
and smelled of flowers.
I was so beautiful.
But these things pass.

—by Eve Bunting

Dressed in beautiful robes and jewels, Heb-Nefert, with her royal husband, led a life of luxury long ago. She was the daughter of a nomarch, a chief magistrate. Now she lies, a mummy, in a glass case for museum visitors to marvel at. These excerpts are from the book *I Am the Mummy Heb-Nefert*, by Eve Bunting. Check it out and read more about the fictitious Heb-Nefert's life.

What HAPPENED *to* GREENLAND'S VIKINGS?

Welcome to the Farm Beneath the Sand. I am Dr. Eric Thorvaldson. I was named after the man who led boats carrying Norse settlers from Iceland to Greenland in about A.D. 985. You may know him as "Eric the Red." I am trying to figure out why the Norse people, who are also known as Vikings, abandoned their settlements here more than 500 years ago.

Look at that sandy shore. In 1990, caribou hunters stumbled on some timbers sticking out of the sandy soil. They told officials at the Greenland National Museum and Archives what they had found, and soon archaeologists began to dig here. They uncovered a house with

WHY IS THIS PLACE CALLED THE FARM BENEATH THE SAND, ERIC?

BECAUSE, TO UNCOVER THESE FARM RUINS, ARCHAEOLOGISTS REMOVED MORE THAN 1,000 TONS OF SAND DEPOSITED BY THAT RIVER OVER THERE.

several rooms. In one of the most important rooms, archaeologists found evidence that the residents engaged in spinning wool and weaving cloth. Archaeologists also discovered evidence of where the residents of this farm kept their animals—mostly sheep and goats, but also some cattle and horses.

If anyone doubted that this was a farm, their noses knew. After the farm was buried in sand, the ground froze, putting the ruins in the deep freeze. When the buildings were uncovered, smells that had been trapped underground for over 500 years were released. From the smell, no one doubted that this was a farm!

How do archaeologists know it was a Viking farm? Excellent question—Greenland's historical

DIG EVEN DEEPER...

NORSE RIDDLE

Sea travel is quite to my liking,
It's so much more pleasant
  than hiking,
Some people call me Norse,
(Hey, I said Norse, not horse),
You can also call
  me a _ _ _ _ _ _.

Answer is on page 212.

records include two long Icelandic stories called
sagas (SAHG uhz), written sometime in the late
1100's or the 1200's. They tell of Eric the Red
and his settlements here. Another book written
in the mid-1200's describes some of the dangers
of the voyage to Greenland, including icebergs
that looked like mountains rising high out of
the sea. In addition, the ruins and artifacts
found here on Greenland look like those found
at Norse settlements in Norway as well as on
Iceland. The Norse settled the island of Iceland
about 100 years before they came to Greenland.

The question that has puzzled historians for
years is: Why did the Vikings leave Greenland?
From about 1000 to the 1200's, as many as
3,000 Norse lived on this island in two main

settlements. Records from those times show that the Greenlanders sent walrus tusks, seal skins, polar bear furs, and falcons to Europe. In return, they got timber, iron, tools, and grain. They needed the timber because Greenland is too cold for large trees to grow. Sometimes the settlers used driftwood to build houses, but they also used the timber to build and repair their houses and ships. Greenlanders needed wheat and other grains, too. The island is so close to the North Pole that it has a very short summer growing season.

In later years, however, something happened. By about 1350, Norse settlers had left one settlement. By 1500, they had left the other. Listen to some theories about what happened to the Norse Greenlanders. Then you can make up your own mind.

THEORY #1

Was Greenland affected by a mini ice age? In the 1990's, scientists drilled ice cores from the icecap in the middle of Greenland. An ice core is a long, narrow plug of ice. It can tell us about climates in past years. Greenland's ice cores showed that the island's climate cooled in the 1300's, especially in the summer months.

Greenland's Norse farmers mainly raised cattle and goats for milk and cheese. They also raised sheep for wool. Clearly, a cooler climate would have meant less hay to feed farm animals during Greenland's long

111

winters. Archaeologists have found evidence of fewer and fewer farm animals in the last years of the settlements.

THEORY #2

Did a major drop in trade with Europe prevent Greenlanders from getting the supplies they needed? Trade records from the 1300's show that the demand for Greenland's products dropped. Also, Norway lost its control over trade routes across the North Atlantic Ocean and stopped sending ships to Greenland. In addition, the cooling climate made the trip to Greenland icier and more dangerous.

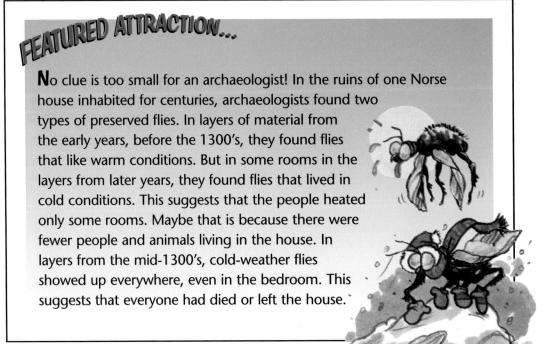

FEATURED ATTRACTION...

No clue is too small for an archaeologist! In the ruins of one Norse house inhabited for centuries, archaeologists found two types of preserved flies. In layers of material from the early years, before the 1300's, they found flies that like warm conditions. But in some rooms in the layers from later years, they found flies that lived in cold conditions. This suggests that the people heated only some rooms. Maybe that is because there were fewer people and animals living in the house. In layers from the mid-1300's, cold-weather flies showed up everywhere, even in the bedroom. This suggests that everyone had died or left the house.

THEORY #3

Did fights with native peoples called Inuit drive the Norse away? Archaeologists have found no evidence for this theory, but Inuit stories tell of some fighting between the two groups. The stories also tell about attacks on the Norse by strangers who arrived in large sailing ships.

THEORY #4

Did the Norse die of starvation or disease? There is no evidence. The remains of the Norse Greenlanders show no signs of sudden, serious starvation. And there are no mass graves. Those are graves containing large numbers of people. Mass graves often date from times of widespread disease, such as plague.

MAYBE THERE WERE FEWER AND FEWER PEOPLE, AND FINALLY THE NORSE GREENLANDERS JUST DIED OUT.

YOU MAY BE RIGHT, AND WE MAY NEVER KNOW FOR SURE. THESE UNSOLVED MYSTERIES MAKE ARCHAEOLOGY FASCINATING!

DIG EVEN DEEPER...

FROZEN IN TIME

Suppose your family and your neighbors suddenly had to leave your homes. Over many years and centuries, the houses were buried in sand or maybe even covered by ice and snow. What if archaeologists found your house hundreds or thousands of years later and sifted through the remains in your room. What could they find out about you?

1. Study the contents of this frozen room. Archaeologist Art T. Fact has tagged artifacts that may be important. Help him interpret the artifacts. Identify each artifact that is labeled and write down what it may tell about the person who occupied the room.

2. Now look again and find an artifact that Art missed. What does that artifact tell you? Can you find more than one missed artifact?

3. If you could actually search this room, where would you look for more artifacts?

Compare your answers with the ones on the bottom of the next page.

ANSWERS

1. Deductions made from artifacts found: (A) The snack shows healthy eating habits. (B) The person had a bird and (C) cat for pets. (D) The person who slept here was a girl. (E) The girl was about 4 feet 10 inches (147 centimeters) tall, so she was probably about 10 or 11 years old. (F) This girl liked animals.

2. Artifacts Art missed: the camera and tennis racket. These items suggest what the girl's hobbies were.

3. Where else to look? Look for film in the camera; files on the computer; contents of the drawers; contents of the part of the closet you cannot see.

Congratulations! You are on your way to becoming a time detective!

Height
4' 10"

A Mummy Walking in the Crypt

A mummy walking in the crypt
Stepped on a banana peel and flipped
Over and over onto its head,
And it would have been killed—
If it hadn't been dead.

—by Paul Duggan

What is the difference between a dead body and a mummy? A mummy is a dead body that has been preserved for hundreds or even thousands of years. Many bodies, such as King Tut's, were treated and dried on purpose. Other bodies were mummified by accident. Nature preserved them. You can read about two such mummies—Ötzi and Juanita—in this chapter.

The MAN from the ICE

From a distance, the two German hikers think the brown object sticking out of a glacier in the Alps is a piece of trash. But as they get closer, they are shocked to discover that it is a frozen body! The hikers guess they have found a fellow hiker who died in an accident a few years or decades earlier.

The hikers quickly return to their inn for help. Over the next few days, police and mountain rescue officers work to recover the body. Freeing the body from the ice is not easy. The workers use ice picks, ski poles, and even a power drill to chip away the ice. The workers are unhappy about the damage they are doing to the body, but they want only to free this poor man from his icy prison. He needs to be identified and buried properly.

As more of the mummy and his belongings are uncovered, some people feel puzzled. This is no ordinary hiker. No modern hiker would be carrying pieces of birch bark or such an unusual ax.

Finally, expert workers carefully free the body from the ice. It is taken to the University of Innsbruck in Austria. There an archaeologist quickly realizes that the "Iceman"

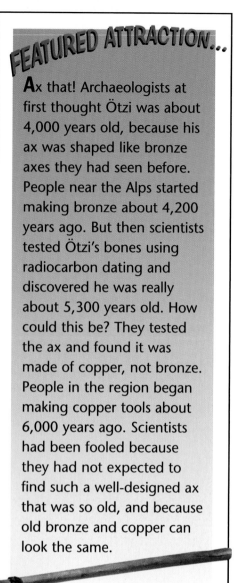

Ax that! Archaeologists at first thought Ötzi was about 4,000 years old, because his ax was shaped like bronze axes they had seen before. People near the Alps started making bronze about 4,200 years ago. But then scientists tested Ötzi's bones using radiocarbon dating and discovered he was really about 5,300 years old. How could this be? They tested the ax and found it was made of copper, not bronze. People in the region began making copper tools about 6,000 years ago. Scientists had been fooled because they had not expected to find such a well-designed ax that was so old, and because old bronze and copper can look the same.

dates back to prehistoric times! The hikers had discovered the mummy of a man who died 5,300 years ago—one of the oldest and best-preserved mummies.

A few days later, a newspaper writer nicknames the mummy "Ötzi" (ERT see) after the Ötztal Alps region near where the mummy was found.

How did Ötzi become a mummy? Scientists believe that snow probably covered Ötzi's body almost immediately after he died, because his remains show no signs of attack by predators. His body quickly froze, and then eventually dried out and became mummified. The cold prevented the body from decaying. Ötzi's body was not crushed because he lay in a ditch and, over the ages, the glacier simply slid over him.

The Iceman's mummy and the artifacts found with him, have revealed some of his secrets, but not all. Where had he come from? Why was he on the mountain? How had he died?

Scientists collected at least several hundred pounds of material, including the remains of many types of plants and animals from the area where the Iceman was found. They also found tiny bits of moss in pieces of the Iceman's clothing. The moss came from the warmer valleys on the Italian side of the Alps, rather than the colder valleys on the Austrian side.

But exactly where in Italy did
Ötzi come from? Scientists found the
answer in the material from the Iceman's
last meal. It contained pollen from
a tree that grows only in certain parts of the
warmer Italian valleys. Groups of that kind
of tree grow in an Italian valley that is within
walking distance of the site where the Iceman
was found! The pollen also told scientists that
the Iceman had died in the spring, when that
tree flowers.

WHERE DID ÖTZI COME FROM?

For ten years, many people believed that
the Iceman had died of exhaustion and cold.
Then in 2001, scientists took three-dimensional
X rays of the Iceman's bones. The images
revealed a stone arrowhead stuck in the
Iceman's left shoulder! The arrow wound
had caused severe bleeding and, finally, death.
The position of the arrowhead proved that
the Iceman had been shot from behind. Did
an enemy stalk him? Was he shot by accident?
We will probably never know.

ARCHAEOLOGISTS THINK HE CAME FROM THE OTHER SIDE OF THE MOUNTAIN.

Based on studies of Ötzi's mummy and artifacts found with him, this is what scientists think the Iceman may have looked like.

SECRETS OF THE ICEMAN

Scientists have learned a great deal about the Iceman by studying his mummy and the artifacts found with him. They have also gained new information about life in Europe 5,300 years ago.

The Iceman stood about 5 feet 3 inches (160 centimeters) tall, based on the overall size of his mummy and the size and strength of his bones. From the wear on his teeth, scientists guessed the Iceman was 40 to 50 years old when he died—very old for that time.

The Iceman's cap (A) was made of bearskin. He wore warm, well-made clothes made of leather, hides, and plant fibers. None of his clothing was woven from thread or yarn. Well-preserved clothing from the Iceman's time had never been found before.

Ötzi wore a long cape (B) made of woven grass. The cape made a good raincoat. He also may have used it as a blanket to sit or sleep on.

Under his cape, Ötzi wore fur clothing (C), including leggings and a long jacket. The top of the jacket did not survive, so scientists do not know if it had sleeves.

His warm, waterproof shoes (D) had bearskin soles and deerskin tops stitched together with cords made of grass. Ötzi stuffed grass into his shoes to keep his feet warm. A cord net fit around Ötzi's foot inside each shoe to hold the grass in place, almost like a sock.

He was armed with a stone knife (E), a copper ax (F), and a 6-foot- (182-centimeters-) long bow (G) and flint-tipped arrows (H). The bow was taller than Ötzi! Other ancient bows found by archaeologists are smooth. But Ötzi's still had rough carving marks and no notches on the ends for the bowstring. So, scientists think Ötzi died before he finished carving the bow. The Iceman also had a lightweight container made of birch bark (I). Archaeologists found charcoal bits in it, which suggests the Iceman carried embers from his fires up the mountain with him.

Testing the material in the Iceman's stomach showed that he had last eaten about eight hours before his death. He had a meal of hard flatbread made from an ancient form of wheat, a green plant, and some meat.

Tests on the Iceman's hair revealed high levels of copper and arsenic. This suggests he may have been involved in making copper, like the copper used in his ax.

One of the Iceman's fingernails, found in the snow, showed that he had suffered from serious illness in the last few months before his death.

121

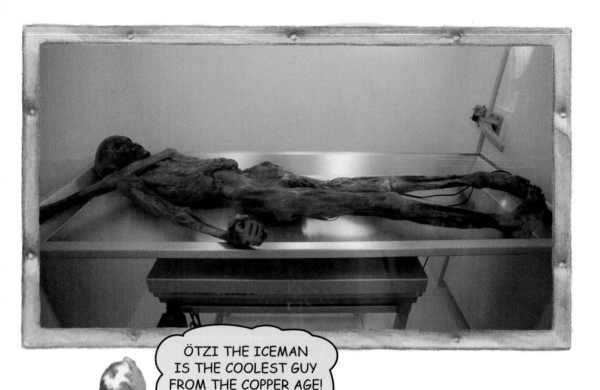

ÖTZI THE ICEMAN IS THE COOLEST GUY FROM THE COPPER AGE!

Today, the Iceman's mummy lies in a special refrigerated room in the South Tyrol Museum of Archaeology in Bolzano, Italy. Visitors may view him through a small window. Scientists also examine him from time to time, but they must be careful. The Iceman's fragile remains can be out of refrigeration for only a very short time. After that, his mummy will begin to thaw and decay.

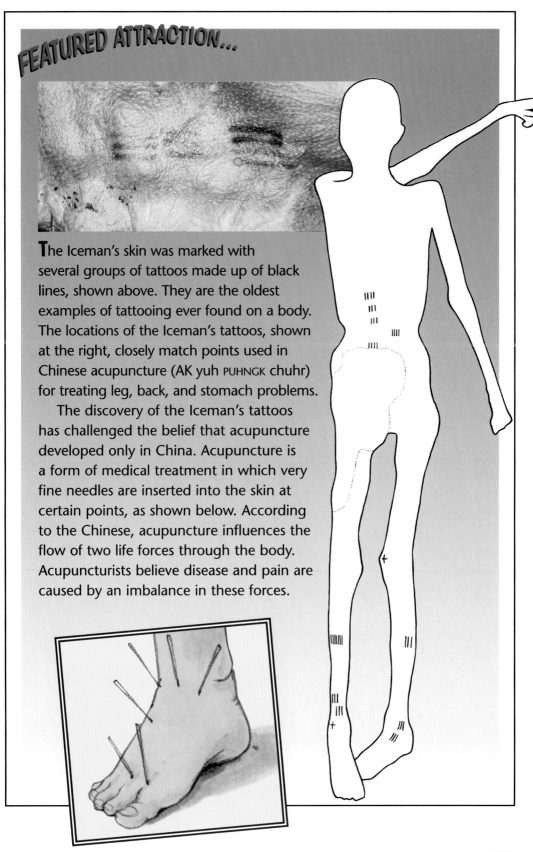

The Iceman's skin was marked with several groups of tattoos made up of black lines, shown above. They are the oldest examples of tattooing ever found on a body. The locations of the Iceman's tattoos, shown at the right, closely match points used in Chinese acupuncture (AK yuh PUHNGK chuhr) for treating leg, back, and stomach problems.

The discovery of the Iceman's tattoos has challenged the belief that acupuncture developed only in China. Acupuncture is a form of medical treatment in which very fine needles are inserted into the skin at certain points, as shown below. According to the Chinese, acupuncture influences the flow of two life forces through the body. Acupuncturists believe disease and pain are caused by an imbalance in these forces.

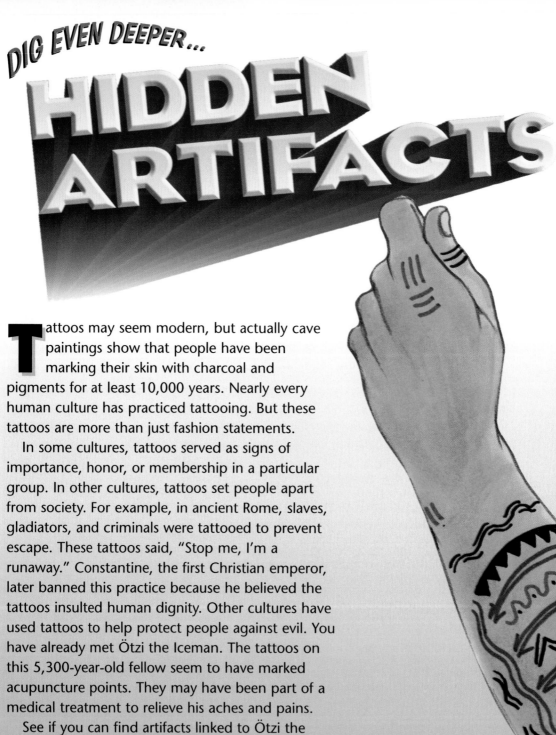

HIDDEN ARTIFACTS

Tattoos may seem modern, but actually cave paintings show that people have been marking their skin with charcoal and pigments for at least 10,000 years. Nearly every human culture has practiced tattooing. But these tattoos are more than just fashion statements.

In some cultures, tattoos served as signs of importance, honor, or membership in a particular group. In other cultures, tattoos set people apart from society. For example, in ancient Rome, slaves, gladiators, and criminals were tattooed to prevent escape. These tattoos said, "Stop me, I'm a runaway." Constantine, the first Christian emperor, later banned this practice because he believed the tattoos insulted human dignity. Other cultures have used tattoos to help protect people against evil. You have already met Ötzi the Iceman. The tattoos on this 5,300-year-old fellow seem to have marked acupuncture points. They may have been part of a medical treatment to relieve his aches and pains.

See if you can find artifacts linked to Ötzi the Iceman in the large tattoo shown here. The answers are on page 212.

ICE MAIDEN of PERU

Dear Diary,
Today, Simon, Joseph, and I saw Juanita, one of the most famous mummies in the world! It is the mummy of an Inca girl. The items found with her suggest she was killed 500 years ago as an offering to the Inca gods in the Andes Mountains of Peru. Her story made us sad, but she and her family probably believed her sacrifice was a great honor.

Juanita is famous because she was the first frozen female mummy ever found in the Andes.

Also, many of her body tissues were frozen. This allowed scientists and medical doctors to examine Juanita's organs and learn more about health and disease in Inca society. Also, from their findings on the mountain, archaeologists could trace for the first time the path followed by Inca priests, sacrificial victims, and other to reach the site where the offering was made.

Juanita was found in September 1995 by American archaeologist Johan Reinhard and Miguel Zárate, his Peruvian climbing companion. They had decided to explore Mount Ampato, because falling ash from a nearby volcano had melted some of the ice and snow there. From historical writings and Inca stories, they also knew that the ancient Inca believed that Mount Ampato was a sacred—holy—place.

The two men were already very tired and hungry when Zárate saw some reddish feathers sticking up out of the snow. (Working at high altitudes, where the air is thin, is exhausting!) The two men discovered that the feathers were part of the headdress of a small Inca statue. Soon they found another statue just like the first. Finally, at the bottom of a steep slope, they found an intriguing bundle.

The bundle was wrapped in brightly colored cloth. It looked like the fabric used to wrap Inca mummies found at other sites in the Andes. The men knew they had found an ancient mummy. Like

Juanita's frozen mummy lay near the top of Mount Ampato, a high volcanic peak.

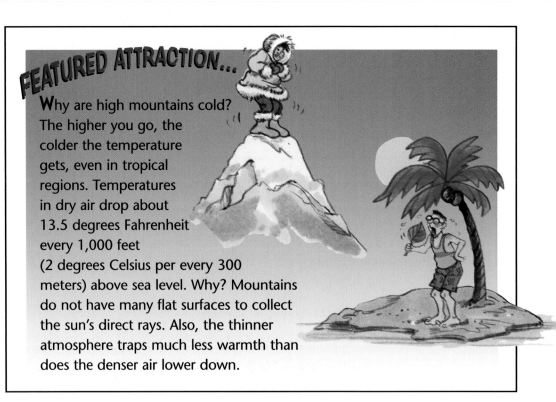

other sacrificial (SAK ruh FISH uhl) mummies found in the Andes, Juanita's mummy had been placed in a platform built high on the rim of the volcano. Reinhard and Zárate could see the remains of the platform above them. But enough ice had melted to tear the platform apart and send the mummy tumbling down the slope. Cloth, bits of pottery, bags containing corn kernels, and another small statue lay near the bundle. The only thing holding the mummy to the mountainside now was ice.

The air was bitterly cold, and darkness was falling. The two men knew they should get back to their camp below. But they were afraid the mummy might roll farther down the slope if they left it where it was. They also worried

that looters might steal it or damage it. Reinhard decided they would take the mummy with them.

They were surprised to discover that the mummy weighed about 80 pounds (36 kilograms). That meant the body was frozen rather than dried out. The worn-out climbers got partway back to camp. However, neither had enough strength left to carry so much weight the rest of the way, so they left the mummy in a protected spot and went back to camp.

In the morning, Reinhard and Zárate were very relieved to find the mummy where they had left it. They carefully carried it down to their camp. To prevent the mummy from thawing out as they walked down

JUANITA'S JOURNEY
Climbing Mount Ampato must have been difficult for Juanita and her group. Archaeologists have found rest stops where they camped. Excavations have uncovered the remains of mat-covered tents, wooden posts that held them up, large stones used as floors, and dried grass used to cushion the floors. All these heavy materials were carried up the mountain on the backs of porters and llamas!

FEATURED ATTRACTION...

Talk about a long-lost relative! Scientists have studied Juanita's DNA, a chemical that helps pass characteristics from one generation to another. The scientists found connections between Juanita and modern Native Americans. Juanita's DNA, like that of other Native Americans, shows links with people from eastern Asia. This supports the theory that the first Americans came from Asia.

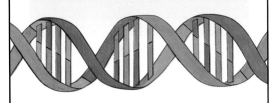

the mountain, Reinhard wrapped it in their foam sleeping pads. These had kept cold air from getting to the men while they slept. In the same way, they kept warm air from getting to the mummy during their thirteen-hour walk to the nearest village. Then the mummy was taken by bus to the city of Arequipa, Peru. There, in the Archaeology Department of Catholic University, it was placed in a refrigerator. The whole trip had taken sixty-four hours, but inside its wraps, the mummy was still safely frozen.

When scientists unwrapped the mummy at the university, they found that she had long, dark hair. She wore a dress with a belt. She also wore a beautiful red shawl fastened by a silver pin. The cold had preserved the fabrics almost perfectly. Some of the tiny statues found near the mummy were dressed in exactly the same way. Each little statue also wore a headdress made of feathers. The archaeologists think Juanita may have, too. It probably fell off her head when she tumbled down the slope.

Scientists have performed many medical tests on the mummy. Three-dimensional X rays of Juanita's skull showed that she had been struck

hard on the head, probably with a club. The
blow had killed her.

Other three-dimensional X rays of her bones
showed that Juanita was about 13 years
old when she died. She had strong
muscles and good teeth. She was
healthy and well fed. She had
eaten vegetables about six or
eight hours before she died.

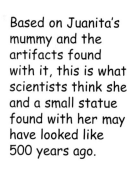

Based on Juanita's
mummy and the
artifacts found
with it, this is what
scientists think she
and a small statue
found with her may
have looked like
500 years ago.

Scientists think Juanita probably came from a wealthy family because she was so healthy and because she was chosen to be a sacrifice in such an important ceremony. She probably lived a very pleasant and comfortable life—until it came to a sudden, violent end.

Juanita has become known as the "Ice Maiden of Peru." Today, she rests in a refrigerated room in Arequipa, Peru.

IN THE SPOTLIGHT...

Ted GOEBEL

SIBERIAN DETECTIVE

When people think of Siberia, they usually think of the middle of nowhere in unbearable cold. But Ted Goebel, shown here on the right, is one archaeologist who thinks otherwise. Since the early 1990's, he and his team have excavated prehistoric animal bones, tools, and charcoal in Siberia. Goebel says these artifacts and ecofacts show us that people have lived in Siberia for tens of thousands of years. He says that these artifacts and ecofacts also may show that the people who lived there were quite handy at hunting and cooking.

The Reason Skeletons Don't Wear Clothes

The reason skeletons don't wear clothes?
Socks won't stay on bony toes,
And underwear just sags and slumps
When hanging from their bony rumps.
Shirts slide off their bony backs,
And pants drop like potato sacks;
And since they can't wear fancy stuff,
Skeletons walk 'round in the buff.

—by Paul Duggan

What is the difference between a skeleton and a mummy? A skeleton is made up only of bones. A mummy contains some of the body's soft tissue, such as skin, muscle, or internal organs. Archaeologists can learn a lot from both skeletons and mummies.

BIRCH-BARK LETTERS

Has your mom or dad ever included one of your drawings in a letter to your grandparents or other relative? About 900 years ago, people did that with letters written on bark. How do we know? They have been uncovered in the Russian city of Novgorod, a modern industrial city that is buried in snow for more than half the year. Within Novgorod is Russia's most important archaeological site. Since 1951, archaeologists have found hundreds of letters there. The letters were all scratched on thin sheets of birch bark using a writing tool

134

made of iron. Then they were rolled into tiny scrolls.

Between the 1000's and the 1500's, the city, which was built mostly of wood, was an important trading center ruled by Viking princes. Many of the birch-bark scrolls are business documents. The letters deal with taxes and orders for goods. Archaeologists also have found school lessons, prayers, magical spells, and a sad love letter.

The birch-bark letters have survived because Novgorod sits on a thick layer of clay. The clay prevents water on the surface from draining deeper into the earth. Novgorod's waterlogged soil has preserved many objects made of wood, leather, and bone.

In addition to the letters, archaeologists have found at least 1,000 wooden and leather toys, dice, an elegant comb made of bone, and many other artifacts. They also have found the well-preserved remains of wooden houses and of miles of log-paved streets the residents of Novgorod built to walk over their spongy ground.

Archaeologists have excavated only a small section of ancient Novgorod. They believe the site may hold at least 20,000 more birch-bark letters!

DIG EVEN DEEPER...
BARKING ORDERS

See what it was like to write birch-bark letters. First, paint the top of a thin piece of balsa wood with brown tempera paint. After the paint dries, scratch words into the surface with a knitting needle. You can scratch an order for a new game or write a sappy love note. How does scratching a letter compare to typing an e-mail note and writing a letter with paper and pen?

Dig this!

This old letter tells what someone was thinking about long ago.

ANGKOR:
The CITY *of* TEMPLES

DAILY DIG

HELP WANTED

Wanted: Archaeologist who wants to

- spend hours in a small vehicle bumping along rough roads;
- hack through dense tangles of jungle vines and plants under hot and very humid conditions;
- travel through areas where bandits lurk.

The rewards include

- discovering temples built by an ancient civilization that is famous for its art and architecture;
- making valuable findings about the development of this civilization and its amazing network of canals.

In the jungle, trees push through and grow over and around ruins. They can easily cover and destroy artifacts. In this photo, a tree's huge roots overtake a building in Angkor.

The information on the opposite page describes a real expedition to the country of Cambodia in Southeast Asia. The destination was Angkor (ANG kohr), the most famous capital city of the Angkor civilization. This civilization was once the most powerful empire in Southeast Asia.

History tells us that Angkor was the most magnificent of all the cities built by the Angkor people between A.D. 820 and the 1100's. The city covered approximately 70 square miles (180 square kilometers). That is about the size of Washington, D.C. About 1 million people may have lived at Angkor. More people lived there than in any European city at that time!

The people of Angkor built many monuments and palaces and at least 100 sandstone temples. The most spectacular is Angkor Wat. This massive temple covers more than 1 square mile (2.6 square kilometers) and is one of the architectural wonders of the world. It was built in the 1100's to honor the Hindu god Vishnu.

By the mid-1400's, war, disease, and political fighting had driven the Angkor people out of their capital. Over the next 400 years, the jungle took over the city. Trees sprang up inside the palaces and temples and broke through the roofs. Huge roots pushed against the buildings, tearing the walls apart.

Over the centuries, explorers occasionally visited Angkor. Some later wrote about it, but few people paid attention to their reports.

Then, in 1860, a French scientist named Henri Mouhot came upon the ruined city. He sketched the buildings and made many notes about the site. Soon afterward, Mouhot died of a disease. This danger still faces archaeologists and other scientists who work in jungles! But Mouhot's writings had attracted the attention of other Europeans. From the 1860's to the mid-1900's, French and Cambodian archaeologists explored and mapped the city. They also restored and rebuilt many of the temples.

Unfortunately, the houses where most of Angkor's people lived have vanished. They were made of wood. Dry climates preserve wood and other organic materials amazingly well. But organic materials usually decay

FEATURED ATTRACTION...

Henri Mouhot's tomb in the jungles of Laos suffered the same fate as the city he rediscovered. Mouhot died in Laos in 1861 and was buried there. In honor of his achievements, the French government erected his tomb in Laos shortly after his death. But jungle plants soon covered it, and people forgot its location. Mouhot's tomb was not rediscovered until 1990.

quickly in hot, moist conditions like the jungles at Angkor.

During the middle to late 1900's, Cambodia was involved in terrible violence and war. In the 1990's, after the fighting calmed, archaeologists were able to return to Angkor. Archaeologist Elizabeth Moore of the University of London led an expedition. Her team became the first to use three-dimensional radar maps of Angkor as a guide. The maps were created from information gathered by a complicated radar system in a high-flying aircraft. Radar maps are particularly useful to archaeologists working in jungles. Radar maps reveal features on the earth's surface that are buried beneath layers of living and decaying plants.

Moore's most exciting discovery lay under a mound spotted by the radar system. When the plants were cleared from the mound, Moore

Radar pictures taken from outer space revealed a huge ancient reservoir, a moat, and more details of Angkor's ancient waterworks. The smaller picture shows a radar picture of a mysterious mound in the jungle. When archaeologists investigated the mound, they found older temples hidden under the vegetation.

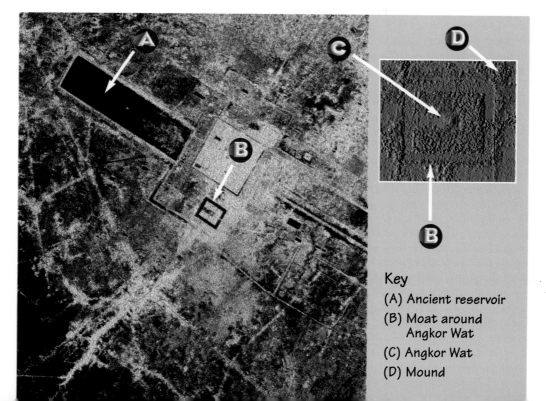

Key
(A) Ancient reservoir
(B) Moat around Angkor Wat
(C) Angkor Wat
(D) Mound

found the ruins of four to six temples. Their design suggests they were built at least 300 years before Angkor Wat. Archaeologists had not realized that people had lived in the area so long ago.

The radar maps also revealed new details about Angkor's amazing waterworks. The city had a system of moats, dikes, rivers, and reservoirs (REHZ uhr vwahrz) that controlled floodwaters during the rainy season and stored water for use during the dry season.

In 1992, the United Nations Educational, Scientific, and Cultural Organization added Angkor to its World Heritage List. The list identifies important places so that they can be preserved for future generations.

After years of clearing away jungle plants and reconstructing ruins, workers restored the ancient temple Angkor Wat.

TRADING at GEDE

This is part of an African ghost town that was abandoned in the 1600's. These ruins show where residents of the city of Gede gathered to pray. Gede, once a rich and beautiful city, is now a national park.

Imagine you are a European explorer in 1450. Now suppose you want to find a sea route to India. That nation's tea, silk, and spices are in great demand in Europe. You spend weeks sailing down the west coast of Africa. The voyage is dangerous, especially as you sail around Africa's southern tip.

As you turn north along Africa's east coast, you get the surprise of your life—a busy port city! Stone buildings line the main street.

This unexplored pillar stands near the ruins of Gede's palace. Archaeologists think it may be a tomb holding the remains of one of the city's holy men.

Africans, Arabs, and people of mixed backgrounds bustle through the streets. You see other traders from lands to the east, especially Indonesia, India, and China. Their ships look very different from yours.

You find a guide to take you inland. There, deep in the forest, you find the prosperous city of Gede (GEH dee). Gede has more than 2,000 people. The rulers live in a cool, comfortable sunken palace. The residents—Muslims who follow the faith of Islam—worship in a stone mosque (mahsk) with an elegant tiled roof. A pillar stands near the palace. You learn later that this is a tomb.

The people here speak Swahili (swah HEE lee), an African language peppered with Arab words. The foreign merchants trade silks, spices, tea, and porcelain—fine china—for valuable ivory and gold from Gede. The goods in the marketplace are of such high quality that hardly anyone wants to trade for the items you are offering. You manage to trade some of the jewelry you brought, however, and you return home with amazing news. East Africa has exciting trade goods!

In later years, European explorers raided Africa's Swahili cities. Gede may have been among them. Some cities were destroyed, and some were abandoned. Still later, some were attacked by people from Somalia. Some cities were wiped out in a different way. Most of the residents were sold into slavery.

When the cities fell into ruin, the forest reclaimed the land. Cloth, carpets, and human remains decayed in the hot, moist climate. But the stones remained, waiting for rediscovery. At last, in the 1920's, settlers found them. And in the late 1940's and 1950's, archaeologists finally began uncovering them.

In Gede, they found a city surrounded by two walls. Inside the walls were wells, homes, shops, and mosques. Archaeologists found washing bowls and rooms for bathing. The thick wall of the sunken palace had pegs for hanging fine carpets. Archaeologists found shell beads, glass beads, gold and silver jewelry, and coins. They also discovered fine Chinese and Arabian porcelain as well as everyday pottery made with local clay.

Their finds helped make Gede a national park in Kenya. The museum there is now a center of study for people who want to learn more about Africa's past.

The SECRETS in CAVES

People have been using caves for shelter and religious ceremonies for hundreds of thousands of years. And because caves are protected from the weather, archaeologists have been finding many of the items people left behind. In fact, archaeologists often find well-preserved artifacts lying in plain sight, just where ancient people left them. Archaeologists also have discovered fabulous works of art in caves as well as some of the most ancient human skeletons ever found. From these discoveries, archaeologists have learned fascinating information about the lives of ancient people.

For example, explorations of caves beneath the ancient Maya city of Dos Pilas in Guatemala have been revealing. They completely changed some archaeologists' ideas about the way the Maya used the caves. Previously, scientists had believed that the pottery, stone blades, bone needles, and human bones found in caves near ancient Maya sites had been left there by the residents. But archaeologist James E. Brady had a different idea. He suggested that the ancient Maya had used the caves for religious ceremonies attended by large numbers of people from the surrounding region. He suggested that the artifacts found in the caves were probably offerings to the gods.

For four years, Brady and his team explored and mapped the caves beneath Dos Pilas. They found twenty-two caves and several miles of underground passages. They also discovered that all the major buildings in Dos Pilas lay above caves. Brady thinks that the ancient Maya built their settlements above and near caves because they believed caves were entrances to the underworld.

Finding caves is not easy in a desert, and especially not in a jungle. Archaeologists often ask local residents for help. They also study an area's geology—its layers of soil and rock. Many caves were formed by streams flowing through soft limestone. Sometimes, archaeologists follow the paths of forest streams to see if they begin or end in a cave. Some archaeologists use aerial photography to look for sinkholes. Sinkholes are openings on the ground that lead to a cave below. Archaeologists also find caves by using satellites. Remote sensing uses satellites that record temperature differences. With remote sensing, archaeologists can locate cool streams flowing from caves into much warmer jungles.

Exploring caves is challenging work. Except for the entrance and the area just inside it, most of a cave is in total darkness. Archaeologists use special lights

FEATURED ATTRACTION...

Has anyone in your family ever lived in a cave? British school teacher Adrian Targett's ancestors did—9,000 years ago! In 1997, scientists identified Targett as a distant relative of a man whose skeleton is the oldest complete skeleton ever found in the United Kingdom. Although many generations separate the two men, Targett's house stands only 100 yards (92 meters) from the entrance to the cave where his ancient ancestor was found!

Once archaeologists walk or crawl beyond the mouth of a cave, they need headlights to see artifacts and ecofacts in the pitch-black darkness.

that do not damage the cave's fragile environment. Also, jagged rocks, uneven floors, and narrow passages make exploration of a cave difficult. Archaeologists have to walk carefully in the dark, cold caves so they do not crush animal bones, bits of wood charcoal, charred nutshells, pottery, or other precious artifacts.

Even traveling to a cave may be difficult. For example, archaeologists recently explored caves in southern Mexico. But the caves are set high in the walls of a canyon. So, the scientists had to float a raft down a shallow river. Then they had to climb up and down steep cliffs to reach the caves.

These caves seemed to be used for ceremonies by the ancient Zoque (SOH kay) people. Inside the caves, archaeologists found woven burial

DIG EVEN DEEPER...

MAKE A CAVE

First, cover your work area with newspaper. Pile several sugar cubes in the shape you would like for the inside of your cave. Mold a block of self-hardening clay around the cubes. Leave at least part of one sugar cube uncovered. This will serve as the opening to the cave. Let the clay dry for several days. Then soak the structure in water. The sugar will dissolve, leaving a hollowed-out space—your cave! If you want, surround your cave with plants, like it is in a jungle. Or, surround it with sand, like a desert cave.

cloths wrapped around the bones of what were probably sacrificial victims. They also found clay jars that may have been used to burn offerings to the gods. The jars contained the remains of incense and food, as well as cloth stained with blood. The blood must have come from people who took part in the ceremonies. In a tropical rain forest, some of these artifacts would have rotted away. But the dry, cool climate in the caves had preserved them all. And the discoveries provided important information about the lives of the ancient Zoque people.

Rock ART

Pictures of hands have been found in rock art around the world, but nobody knows what the hands mean. This photo shows prehistoric rock art that was found in a cave in Queensland, Australia.

Archaeologists duck and squeeze between the rocky walls of a cave. Suddenly, they see flashes of color—bright red, brown, black, yellow, and a little bit of white. In the flickering light, animals appear to be jumping out of the walls! The ancient people who used this cave left amazing artworks behind.

The oldest pictures ever found are on the walls of caves, cliffs, and other rock formations. This form of art, called rock art, has been found all over the world. But the best-preserved rock art is in well-protected areas, especially in dry climates. Rock-art sites have been discovered by archaeologists, as well as by farmers, hunters, and hikers. Some important cave art has been found by children, too.

If you look closely at rock art, you will see that the ancient artists used a variety of techniques to create their pictures. Some artworks are engravings (ehn GRAYV ihngz). Some are paintings.

Ancient artists made rock engravings by using something such as a stone or an antler to scratch, cut, or poke holes into soft rock. The engravings are called petroglyphs (PEHT ruh glihfs). Many petroglyphs have been found in sandstone and limestone.

To make rock paintings, artists applied colors to rocks. Rock paintings are called pictographs (PIHK tuh grafs). Ancient paints came from materials found in nature. For example, the artists ground up plants, minerals, or colored rocks and mixed them with vegetable oil or animal fat to make them stick to the rock. Black paint was often made from charcoal. Painters sometimes mixed their colors with saliva and then spit the mixture onto the wall or blew it through a tube. That is why some paintings look cloudy or as if they were spray-painted. Other painters

BREAKING DOWN THE WORDS CAN HELP YOU REMEMBER WHAT THEY MEAN. PETROGLYPH: *PETRO* MEANS "ROCK," AND *GLYPH* MEANS "CARVED WORK."

PICTOGRAPH: *PICTO* MEANS "TO PAINT," AND *GRAPH* MEANS "TO WRITE."

WHY DID ANCIENT ARTISTS MAKE PICTURES ON ROCKS?

used their fingers or brushes made from animal hair. Some used the fringed ends of plant stems or wooden sticks. Some colors appear to have been dabbed onto the rock with a pad. Archaeologists have even found ancient "crayons" made of a colored earth or clay called ocher (OH kuhr).

Rock art is especially important to archaeologists who study prehistoric people, because most rock art was created long before writing systems existed. These ancient people left no written records about their way of life, customs, or beliefs.

Archaeologists and other scholars have different ideas about what the pictures may have meant. Some people think rock art was used as a sign to mark a group's territory—such as "No Trespassing" or "We Are Here." Other

Once a desert, not always a desert— rock art sometimes provides clues about the environment of the prehistoric artists. Today, the Sahara is a huge desert. But rock art found in the mountains of the central Sahara from about 4000 B.C. and earlier shows a lush landscape with forests, lakes, and grasslands. The images also show an amazing variety of animals, including ostriches, giraffes, elephants, crocodiles, fish, and even an extinct kind of water buffalo!

prehistoric pictures seem to tell stories or record important events. On several cave walls in India, harpists play musical instruments for slender dancers who are wearing skirts and headdresses. Could these images be the history of a celebration?

For many years, scholars believed that the artworks found in European caves were magical symbols, intended to help hunters find their prey. Then some archaeologists compared the animals in the paintings to the animal bones discovered at prehistoric campsites. They learned that prehistoric artists did not usually eat the animals they drew. Some scholars said that prehistoric Europeans used cave art to mark the passing of time. Other scholars said that the art was used in ceremonies and rituals.

Recently, some archaeologists have argued that the images represent visions seen by religious leaders called shamans (SHAH muhnz) during trances or dreams. Some cultures believe shamans have powers that come from direct contact with the spirit world. According to these legends, shamans enter the supernatural world to cast out evil spirits, heal the sick, and otherwise help members of their group. Each culture may have had its own meanings for its drawings. We will probably never know for sure.

Sometimes, archaeologists find clues to the meaning of rock art in stories handed down from generation to generation. From southwestern North America to northwestern South America, one of the most common

Kokopelli figures on a rock in New Mexico

images in rock art is a figure that looks a lot like a flute player. He usually has spikes on his head and a rounded back that could be a hump or a backpack. Sometimes, he wears a sash or a kilt. He is also portrayed as an insect with a long snout!

Native Americans have different legends for this figure, who is often called Kokopelli. One Hopi legend says Kokopelli carries corn seeds in his pack and plays his flute to help the seeds grow. Some people of the Andes Mountains believe the

This petroglyph of two giraffes is the largest and one of the most beautiful in Africa. The larger giraffe is about 20 feet (6 meters) tall. They were etched in the Sahara about 6,000 to 9,000 years ago.

figure is a wandering medicine man whose flute music heals the sick. Some scholars believe Kokopelli may have originated in Central America or even farther south. Traders traveling from village to village in that area often announced their arrival by playing the flute.

Rock art can be difficult to date. It is not usually buried, so stratigraphy—the study of the layers of rock and earth—can tell us nothing about the age of the rock art. And petroglyphs contain no organic materials, so

For more than 900 years, people have left their mark on this rock in Utah. What pictures do you see on this rock?

Many rock art images are in danger. Sometimes, rocks crack because of temperature changes or because of plants growing over them. And sometimes people destroy or damage images just by touching them. Around the world, people are restoring rock art the way this woman is. Other people are recording as much rock art as they can. They are making scaled drawings, watercolors, and photos of rock art so that we will have a permanent record of these amazing images.

radiocarbon dating cannot be used to figure out their age. However, radiocarbon dating may reveal how old pictographs are. Scientists can measure the amount of carbon in the charcoal, vegetable oils, and animal fats that were used to make the ancient paints.

Archaeologists may date an image by comparing its style to images whose age is already known. Excavation of artifacts above, beneath, or around the rock art also may reveal clues to the age of the art. Remember, though, these items may not have been used by the people who made the rock art.

ONE CANYON

MANY CULTURES!

Sego Canyon sits in central Utah. Over thousands of years, many cultures have lived there, and they have left artifacts that prove it! For example, the canyon walls are decorated with rock art from three Native American cultures. There are huge pictures of horses, buffalo, and mountain sheep that people drew some 1,500 years ago. There are also humanlike figures that have huge eyes and antennae. These sandstone cliffs may have been an ancient art gallery or a holy place. No one knows for sure.

Proof of previous inhabitants can also be found in Sego's ghost town. It holds artifacts left by people in the more recent past. Ghost towns are found throughout the United States and Canada, but those in the American West are the most famous. During the 1800's, discoveries of rich deposits of

Find a pigment, such as soft stones, dried clay, or freeze-dried berries. Next, use a small rock to crush some pigment on a hard, flat rock. Crush until it becomes a powder. Now, choose a liquid—water, vegetable oil, or glue. Mix the liquid and pigment in a jar lid until it is as thick as paint. Use your finger or a stick to draw a picture of an animal on a piece of brown paper. Crumple the paper to make it look like a real rock!

gold, silver, and copper lured crowds of would-be miners westward. Soon, primitive towns sprang up with shacks, saloons, and sometimes a church. After the mines were used up or metal prices fell, the people moved to new places to make money, leaving the towns and the mines behind. The dry mountain air has preserved many of the ghost towns' wooden buildings, but wind and windblown dirt have sanded away the paint.

During the early 1900's, people moved to Sego because of coal, not precious metals. Unfortunately, the water supply for the town and the coal mine soon began to dry up, and in 1947, the mine was closed. Today, visitors can see the remains of the town's railroad, a cemetery, and a number of abandoned buildings, including a general store, a boarding house, and some other houses. Many visitors photograph the ghostly site and try to imagine what the town was like full of life.

Much of Sego's ghost town has worn away, but luckily, these huge, ancient pictures haven't!

Writing ROCKS!

Epigraphers (ih PIHG ruh fuhrz) specialize in reading ancient writings. Why read all day when you could be out digging? Well, epigraphers do exciting work. For one thing, they are not interested in writing that appears on paper. No, they study writing on objects, such as stone, pottery, metal, and bone.

Figuring out what ancient writings mean is like working on secret codes. Epigraphers try one meaning after another until bit by bit they decipher (dih SY fer) an ancient message.

LOOK AT THE
WRITING ON
THIS WALL!
IT ROCKS!

Epigraphers work with archaeologists who are experts in other fields, too. Imagine you are on a dig in southern Iraq, in southwestern Asia. Thousands of years ago, this area was known as the ancient region of Sumer (SOO muhr). One day, you dig up some clay tiles with writing on them. What do you think happens next?

First, you call a scientist who is an expert with plant remains, an archaeobotanist. This scientist takes a sample of dirt from where the tile was found and puts it in a special tub of water. Plant pollen and other bits float to the surface. The specialist collects the floating material and studies it to learn what plants grew or were used in the area.

Next, you share your clay tile with a ceramic technologist. That's a clay expert. You can learn what kind of clay was used, when it was used, and which group of people made the tile.

Then the real detective work begins. You try to find out who was saying what to whom.

Luckily, the people in Sumer kept records. They used a wedge-shaped pen, called a stylus (STY luhs), to make impressions on clay tablets. We call that kind of writing cuneiform (kyoo NEE uh fawrm), or wedge-shaped writing. Thanks to cuneiform writing, we know many details about business and trade in ancient Sumer.

EPIGRAPHERS' WORK SOUNDS LIKE FUN. AND IT IS IMPORTANT, TOO. IF IT WEREN'T FOR WRITING LIKE THE CUNEIFORM ON THIS CLAY TABLET, WE WOULD HARDLY KNOW ANYTHING ABOUT LIFE IN SUMER OR ANCIENT EGYPT!

Egyptian writing called hieroglyphics
(HI uhr uh GLIHF ihks) tells us even more.
It presents a dramatic picture of
Egyptian life—from royalty to
slaves. For a long time, these
details were literally locked in a
stone tablet called the
Rosetta stone. No one really
knew how the ancient
Egyptians lived. All we had
were objects, pictures,
monuments—and guesses.
And then in the early
1800's, the writing on the
Rosetta stone was decoded!

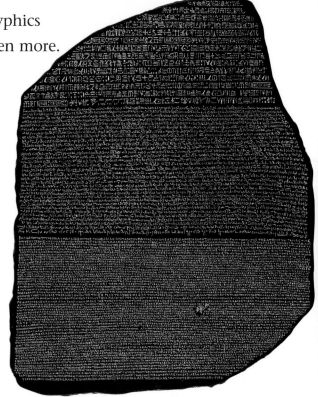

Rosetta stone

How could one rock carry
so much important information? Well, it is not
so much what the writing said as the way it was
written. You see, many ancient people carved
important information on large stones called
stelae (STEE lee). But for 1,400 years, no one
could read the words on Egyptian stelae. That's
because they were written in hieroglyphics.

Hieroglyphs are word pictures. Most people
thought that each hieroglyph stood for a word,
an object, or an idea. Some thought they might
be symbols of sounds. Look at this picture:

Some scholars thought this sign must mean "eagle" or "bird." Still others thought it might stand for the qualities an eagle possesses, such as strength or good vision. A few thought it might stand for a sound in the ancient Egyptian word for "eagle." But no one knew for sure.

Then in 1799, an officer in the French army found a stele near the town of Rosetta, in Egypt. Like other stelae, it had a message on it. But this message was repeated three times. The Rosetta stone was inscribed in hieroglyphics; in everyday demotic (dih MAHT ihk) Egyptian; and—here's the breakthrough—in Greek!

Scholar after scholar tried to decode the hieroglyphs, but no one had much success. Then a young French scholar named Jean François Champollion gave it a try. Like many scholars of his time, Champollion knew English, German, and Italian. He also learned Arabic, Greek, Hebrew, Latin, Persian, Sanskrit, and Coptic—an Egyptian language that used Greek letters.

THE SCHOLARS ALREADY KNEW GREEK, SO THEY KNEW WHAT THE MESSAGE SAID. ALL THEY HAD TO DO WAS FIGURE OUT HOW TO TRANSLATE THE HIEROGLYPHS!

FEATURED ATTRACTION...

thehieroglyphicanddemoticwritingontherosetta stoneincludednopunctuationorspacesbetween wordsthatmadethemveryhardtodecodeandread!

FEATURED ATTRACTION...

Left—right—left—some hieroglyphs are read from left to right. Others are read from right to left, or from top to bottom, or even in a circle. To figure out how to read them, scholars look at the way the people, animals, and other symbols are facing.

For more than ten years, Champollion spent all his spare time studying the message on the Rosetta stone. He finally figured out that most of the hieroglyphs on the stone stood for sounds as well as objects. For example, here are the hieroglyphs and letter names for two great Egyptian rulers—Ptolemy and Cleopatra:

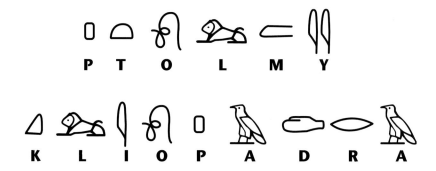

In 1822, Champollion published a pamphlet on his discovery. He explained that earlier scholars had not been wrong. They just had not realized that Egyptian hieroglyphs stood for

WOW! SOME HIEROGLYPHS LOOK A LOT LIKE THESE CHINESE CHARACTERS. THIS POEM WAS INSCRIBED ON WOOD ABOUT 2,000 YEARS AGO. PAPER WAS RARE AT THAT TIME.

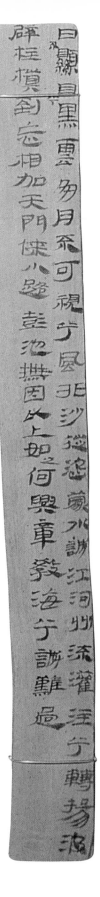

sounds as well as for objects and ideas. So scholars could finally read these ancient writings.

Chinese writing is the oldest form of writing still in use. It has not changed much in thousands of years. For example, the ancient character that means "man" has been simplified and is still used today.

You may think that after all these years of successful decoding, epigraphers in China and elsewhere have it easy nowadays. But that is not true. Many puzzles and mysteries remain.

Written languages usually change over time. For example, Europe alone has had dozens of alphabets. Archaeologists working with European languages almost always have some translating and decoding to do.

Also, many forms of writing have never been decoded. For example, epigraphers have not made much progress deciphering the writing from the Indus Valley in India and Pakistan. This is mainly because the inscriptions found there are so short.

No one knows what most rock art means either, but we can keep looking for clues!

Linda Schele was an artist, a teacher—and a codebreaker. She was born in Tennessee in 1942 and died in 1998. Schele was first captivated by the Maya people when she visited the Palenque ruins in Mexico. Long ago, the Maya were conquered. Their alphabet was forbidden. Most of their literature and written documents were destroyed. People were made to read, write, and speak a new language. Though some writing survived, the ancient Maya language eventually became a mystery. In the late 1980's, by working with the modern Maya people of Mexico and Guatemala, Schele began to see links between the Indian people's culture and their ancient past. Schele used her artist's skills and studied Maya art, language, writing, and archaeology. She helped break the code of the Maya's hieroglyphics. This gave today's Maya the tools they needed to learn more about their history.

Linda
SCHELE
CODEBREAKER

Skeleton Key

Does it open a house with a tombstone door
and spiderwebs on the marble floor
under a slab by a graveyard tree—
Is that why they call it a skeleton key?

Do skeletons use them to play their bones,
tapping out tunes on xylophones
made of rows of ribs and knobby knees—
Is that why they call them skeleton keys?

Does a skeleton key open any door
(like mine) at night, when it's hours before
anyone wakes, when no one sees
do they rattle around wherever they please—
Is that why they call them skeleton keys?

—by Alice Schertle

The word *skeleton* comes from Greek words meaning "dried-up body." A skeleton key is a "barebones" kind of key that can open many locks. The term was first used in the early 1800's to refer to a plain, thin key that had no notches or special cuttings. But where did that key get its spooky name? Here's one writer's creepy thoughts on the mystery.

Skyline on the Sea Floor

an tapped Sanjay as the two boys got
off the school bus. "Meet me at the
club," he whispered. "Tell the others."

Dan hurried to the clubhouse, an old shed.
A sign over the door read "ELM STREET
DETECTIVES." But the only mystery the club
had solved lately was finding a lost dog.

Soon Sanjay, Emma, and Kendra showed up.
"What's going on?" they asked.

I THINK WE MAY HAVE BEEN LOOKING IN THE WRONG PLACES FOR OUR MYSTERIES. I HAVE SOME INFORMATION ON UNDERWATER EXCAVATIONS!

This artist's drawing of Alexandria 2,000 years ago shows the view along one of the main thoroughfares. The beautiful city had wide streets, fine buildings, gardens, and plazas. Alexandria was founded in 331 B.C. by Alexander the Great.

Dan grinned, "The historical museum where my mom works is putting together a big exhibit (ehg ZIHB iht) on underwater archaeology."

"Did you know that archaeologists could not work very well underwater until the 1930's?" said Kendra. "Before that, when a ship like the *Titanic* sank, people did not have high-tech equipment to help recover it. Today, archaeologists have scuba (SKOO buh) gear, submersibles (suhb MUR suh buhlz), and even robots to help them explore underwater."

"So is underwater archaeology all about finding shipwrecks?" Sanjay asked.

"Sometimes," Dan said, "archaeologists dig up other things, like sunken cities."

Dan unfolded a packet of papers. "Here is a map of the harbor area of ancient Alexandria

FEATURED ATTRACTION...

Underwater archaeologists use portable air tanks, diving bells, submersibles, and robots. But in the A.D. 1700's, a high-tech diving machine was made of a barrel and rope, as re-created in this photo. A diver in the air-tight barrel could be lowered by a heavy rope about 60 feet (18 meters). The barrel had enough air for half an hour. The diver, whose arms were outside the barrel, could look through a glass window and send simple signals to people on the surface by tugging on another rope.

I THOUGHT THE LIGHTHOUSE WAS BUILT ON AN ISLAND.

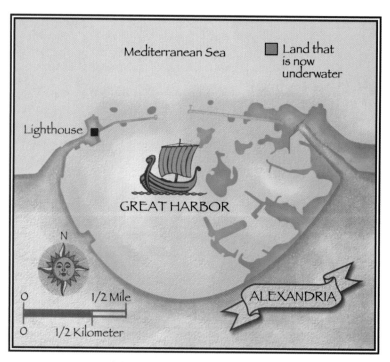

Mediterranean Sea

Land that is now underwater

Lighthouse

GREAT HARBOR

N

0   1/2 Mile

0   1/2 Kilometer

ALEXANDRIA

IT WAS! THE ISLAND IS NOW CONNECTED TO THE MAINLAND. OTHER PARTS OF ALEXANDRIA SANK INTO THE SEA HUNDREDS OF YEARS AGO.

in Egypt," he said. The others moved closer to take a look. "How could part of a city sink?" asked Sanjay.

"Earthquakes," Dan explained. "Egypt has had a lot of big ones. Parts of Alexandria have slipped as much as 20 feet (6 meters) into the ocean. Here is the story about how archaeologists found the lighthouse."

For centuries, people have told stories about the amazing structures called the Seven Wonders of the Ancient World. Six of the Seven Wonders of the Ancient World have now disappeared. Only the pyramids at Giza in Egypt remain. But a team of Egyptian and French archaeologists believe they have found the ruins of another one of the wonders—the Lighthouse of Alexandria. Sometimes the lighthouse is called the Pharos of Alexandria, after the island it was built on.

Archaeologists already knew a great deal about the lighthouse from ancient writings. They knew it had been built around 280 B.C. They knew that it was about the height of a modern 40-story building and that it rose from a stone platform in three parts. The bottom part was square. The middle had eight sides. The top was circular. According to ancient accounts, a fire burning at the top of the lighthouse provided light. Archaeologists also knew that a major earthquake severely damaged the lighthouse in A.D. 1303. Another earthquake in 1349 completely destroyed it.

Archaeologists suspected that some ruins from the lighthouse might still survive under the harbor of modern Alexandria. But they had no way of finding out for many years. One reason was the harbor's murky water. Because of high pollution levels, divers could see only several feet in front of them. In addition, the Egyptian government had banned diving in the harbor to help protect the area against enemy attack.

In 1960, however, an Egyptian archaeologist named Kamal Abu el-Saadat won permission to dive in the harbor. Over the next few years, he found many ancient artifacts, including a huge stone statue of an Egyptian goddess. It had been made around the same time as the lighthouse. Now archaeologists were sure that valuable artifacts lay underwater in the harbor!

Since the 1990's, French archaeologists Franck Goddio and Jean-Yves Empereur have been exploring the harbor. They are using new

A diver examines an ancient sphinx on the ocean floor just outside the harbor of Alexandria.

and expensive technologies. For example, they have surveyed the harbor floor with sonar (SOH nahr) devices. These send out sound waves and receive echoes after the waves bounce off an object. The archaeologists also use highly sensitive magnetometers (MAG nuh TAHM uh turz) to locate buried iron objects.

Their most useful tool, however, is called the Global Positioning System, or GPS for short. The GPS is used in cars, boats, and handheld computers. GPS receivers use satellites in outer space to determine the exact location of a person or object on the earth. The GPS helps map places that are hard to map using other surveying methods. With the GPS, the archaeologists have made extremely accurate maps of objects lying in the harbor.

With the Global Positioning System, a diver maps the location of a sphinx. Because the satellite signals do not penetrate water, the receivers being carried to the sea floor must be linked to floating antennas.

Here, an archaeologist measures a large granite piece that once decorated the lighthouse.

The archaeological teams dive into the murky waters in wet suits. They take pictures of the relics and map their locations. The divers have discovered many statues on the harbor floor, mostly stone sphinxes (SFINGKS uhz). A sphinx is an imaginary creature. The Egyptian government is so pleased that it has provided money so that some of the statues can be preserved for an underwater museum.

Most exciting of all, the teams found thousands of pillars and giant stone blocks. Some of the blocks are 36 feet (11 meters) long and weigh 83 tons. Interestingly, some blocks look like they fit together. The archaeologists concluded that these blocks were once part of even bigger blocks that had cracked apart. They decided that only one building in ancient Alexandria could have been built with such large blocks—its famous lighthouse.

More support for this theory came from a map showing the location of the pillars and blocks. Archaeologists discovered that the largest blocks lie along a line that pointed out to sea. They concluded that there could be only one explanation for this pattern—the blocks fell into the harbor all at once and from the same direction. A strong earthquake could have sent the lighthouse's blocks tumbling in this way.

The colossal torso of a statue is eased onto a dock after being lifted from the sea floor. The statue shows a Ptolemic king dressed as an Egyptian pharaoh. It once stood outside Alexandria's lighthouse.

WONDER-FUL

The Seven Wonders of the Ancient World were called wonders because of their impressive size or some other unusual feature. The Lighthouse of Alexandria was one of these ancient wonders. Can you match the other six?

1. The pyramids of Egypt at Giza (GEE zuh)

2. The Hanging Gardens of Babylon (BAB uh luhn)

3. The Temple of Artemis at Ephesus (EHF ih suhs)

4. The statue of Zeus at Olympia

5. The Mausoleum (MAW suh LEE uhm) at Halicarnassus (hal ih kahr NAS uhs)

6. The Colossus (kuh LAHS uhs) of Rhodes

ANSWERS: A 3, B 1, C 5, D 2, E 4, F 6.

The WORLD'S OLDEST TREASURE SHIP

THIS SHIP MODEL IS PRETTY COOL.

HEY, CAN WE FINALLY HEAR ABOUT A SUNKEN SHIP?

Here is the story of one of the oldest and most important shipwrecks ever found. It is much older than the sunken city of Alexandria. This shipwreck is about 3,300 years old.

"Metal biscuits with ears." That is how a sponge diver described some oddly shaped objects he saw on the floor of the Mediterranean Sea at Ulu Burun (oo loo boo ruhn) on the coast of southern Turkey. When American archaeologist George F. Bass dived there, he became very excited. He discovered that the "biscuits" were actually flat, rectangular ingots—blocks—of copper. The "ears" were the handles used for carrying the ingots. The ship also carried a considerable amount of tin.

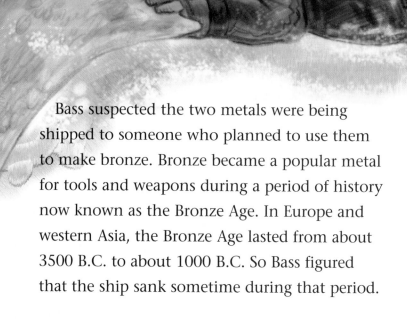

Bass suspected the two metals were being shipped to someone who planned to use them to make bronze. Bronze became a popular metal for tools and weapons during a period of history now known as the Bronze Age. In Europe and western Asia, the Bronze Age lasted from about 3500 B.C. to about 1000 B.C. So Bass figured that the ship sank sometime during that period.

From A.D. 1984 to A.D. 1994, Bass and his team explored and excavated the shipwreck. The work was hard and dangerous. No archaeologists had ever worked that far below the surface—145 to 200 feet (45 to 61 meters)—using only scuba gear. The divers could stay down for only twenty minutes at a time. They were allowed to dive just twice a day. Together, they made more than 20,000 dives.

FEATURED ATTRACTION...

Prepared for pirates? In addition to precious cargo, archaeologists found daggers, swords, spearheads, and other weapons in the shipwreck at Ulu Burun. Did the people on the ship intend to trade these weapons? Or were they the ship's weapons against pirates who hoped to steal their treasures?

Most of the objects that survived in the water at Ulu Burun are made of pottery, glass, precious stones, ivory, or precious metals. Many were everyday items. Above are a cup and jar from Greece. The fancy ivory handle, right, shows a body bent over like an acrobat. What do you suppose the handle was attached to?

The results of the excavation were astonishing. Bass's team brought up about 18,000 artifacts from one of the largest and richest ancient cargoes ever found. The artifacts revealed that international trade during the Bronze Age involved many more countries than historians had thought.

The team identified where many of the artifacts found in the shipwreck were from by looking at the material they were made of and studying the designs on them. Bass's team found many items from countries bordering

Mediterranean comes from Latin words meaning "center of the world." Long before airplanes were invented, people traveled over the seas in boats. Some of the first sea exploration was made by sailors from lands bordering the Mediterranean. That sea was the center of their world. The wreck at Ulu Burun proved just how far Mediterranean explorers were traveling at the time the ship sank thousands of years ago. This map shows how people on the ship could have reached many lands and traded with many people by sailing the Mediterranean.

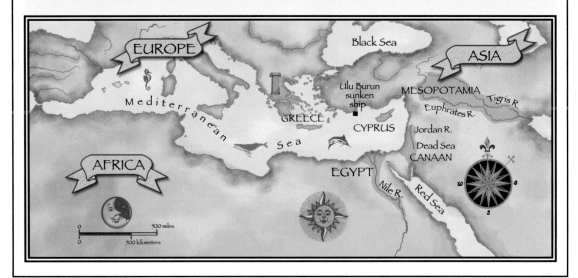

the Mediterranean Sea. These included bronze swords and jewelry from a country called Canaan (now part of Egypt, Israel, and Jordan); pottery from the island of Cyprus; glass beads from Greece; and gold and silver charms from Egypt. One of the gold charms had the name of Queen Nefertiti of Egypt on it. The archaeologists also found a stone with a design on it. This object, called a seal, was used to stamp the design on objects. The seal had been carved in Mesopotamia (now part of Iraq, Syria, and Turkey). They even found a kind of notebook. It was made of two wooden "pages" joined with an ivory hinge. As shown below, the insides of the pages originally had been covered with wax for use as a writing surface, but none of the wax had survived.

Many items came from much farther away. The archaeologists found logs of precious wood from central Africa and amber beads from northern Europe. These discoveries showed that Bronze Age traders must have had contact with people beyond the Mediterranean in their search for trade goods.

Archaeologists used a technique called tree ring dating to determine when the ship sank.

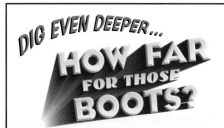

DIG EVEN DEEPER...

HOW FAR FOR THOSE BOOTS?

Where does your family buy shoes, boots, shirts, and toys? Long before there were discount malls, people traded goods for the things they needed. The people on the ship found at Ulu Burun traveled far to gather their cargo. Archaeologists think this bronze goddess found with the ship may have come from Syria, because it looks like other figurines that were made there. Her head, hands, and feet are covered in gold. She may have been the ship's protective goddess. Read tags, labels, and packaging to find out where the items in your house came from. Which was made farthest from your home?

They examined the pattern of tree rings in a piece of firewood found in the wreckage. They found that the firewood came from a tree that had been cut down sometime before 1300 B.C. They believe the ship sank shortly after that.

The discovery of the shipwreck at Ulu Burun has added greatly to our knowledge of the Bronze Age. The ship was not only a treasure trove of gold and silver and other valuables, but also a bank of knowledge about an important period in history.

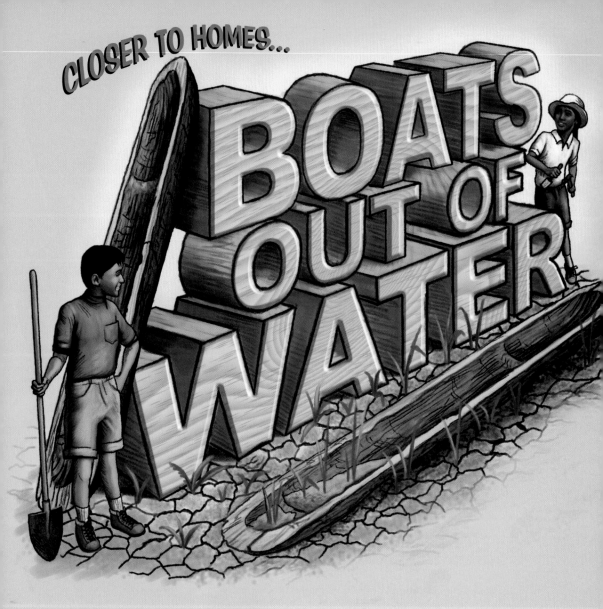

BOATS OUT OF WATER

Not every underwater excavation takes place far out at sea. Some are carried out near cities and towns. Recently, a group of high school students and volunteers helped make an amazing underwater find right in the city of Gainesville, Florida.

In the spring and summer of 2000, Florida was suffering from a long period of dry weather called a drought (drowt). Because so little rain fell, many streams, lakes, and ponds started to dry up. One day, some high school students were working on a school project near a dry lake

190

bed. They saw old-looking dugout canoes sticking out of the mud. The remains showed that the wooden canoes had been big. The shortest was 15 feet (4.5 meters) long, and the longest was 31 feet (9.5 meters) long.

Archaeologists came to study the canoes. They estimated that the oldest canoes ranged from about 1,000 years old to 3,000 years old. These canoes—more than 80 of them—may be the single most important discovery of Native American canoes ever made in North America.

Dugout canoes were—and still are— a popular form of transportation in several parts of the world. Typically, one canoe is made from a whole tree trunk. In some cultures, people hollow out the trunk by carving the wood down the middle. Native Americans, however, made the canoes found in Florida by burning out the middle of the tree trunks. The Native Americans then scooped out the charred wood with tools made of stone or shell.

If you ever see something that looks interesting and historical along a lake or ocean, don't move it! Report your discovery to a park ranger, a local historical society, or the police. Artifacts sometimes wash ashore from shipwrecks that are lying in deeper water. But collecting artifacts is illegal along most public shores.

DIG EVEN DEEPER...

EXCAVATE with EXPERTS

Take part in a real excavation, like the one shown here where people are digging up canoes in Florida! Help experts decide where to dig. Give your ideas about what their findings might mean. Many archaeologists in the field connect online to classrooms around the world. Their teams send daily journals to the students. The students ask questions and help direct the dig! Ask your teacher to check out Web sites. One is www.quest.classroom.com.

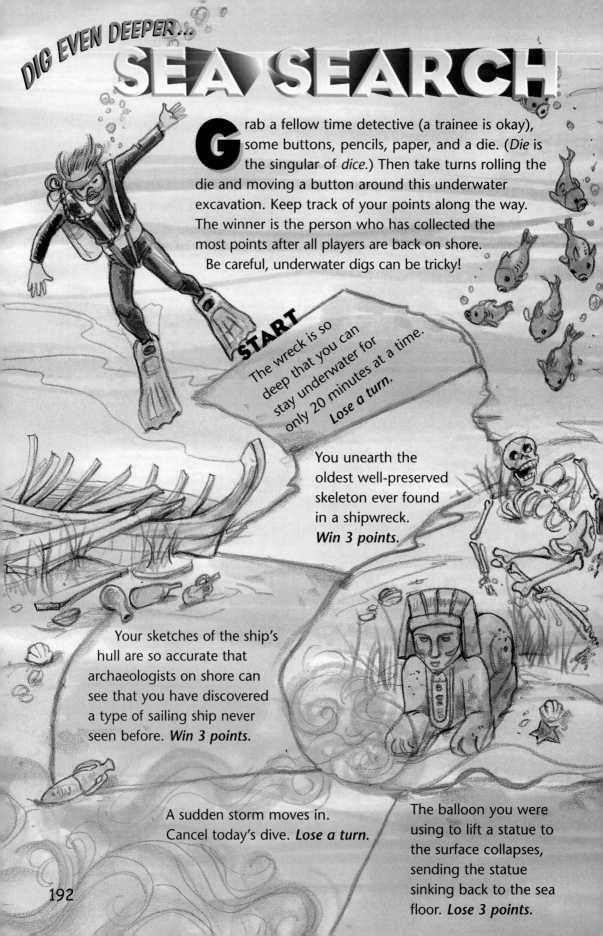

SEA SEARCH

Grab a fellow time detective (a trainee is okay), some buttons, pencils, paper, and a die. (*Die* is the singular of *dice*.) Then take turns rolling the die and moving a button around this underwater excavation. Keep track of your points along the way. The winner is the person who has collected the most points after all players are back on shore. Be careful, underwater digs can be tricky!

START

The wreck is so deep that you can stay underwater for only 20 minutes at a time. *Lose a turn.*

You unearth the oldest well-preserved skeleton ever found in a shipwreck. *Win 3 points.*

Your sketches of the ship's hull are so accurate that archaeologists on shore can see that you have discovered a type of sailing ship never seen before. *Win 3 points.*

A sudden storm moves in. Cancel today's dive. *Lose a turn.*

The balloon you were using to lift a statue to the surface collapses, sending the statue sinking back to the sea floor. *Lose 3 points.*

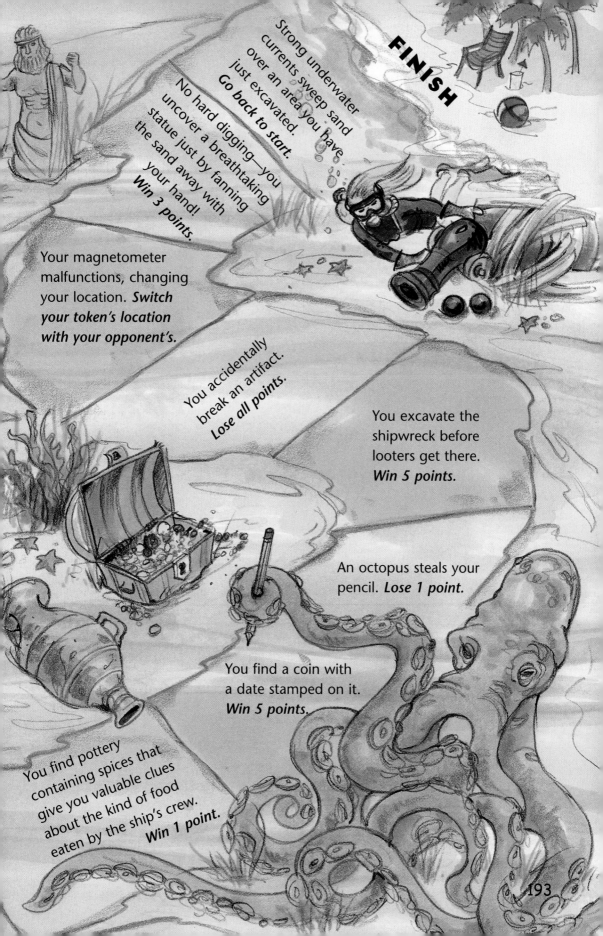

FINISH

Strong underwater currents sweep sand over an area you have just excavated. **Go back to start.**

No hard digging—you uncover a breathtaking statue just by fanning the sand away with your hand! **Win 3 points.**

Your magnetometer malfunctions, changing your location. *Switch your token's location with your opponent's.*

You accidentally break an artifact. *Lose all points.*

You excavate the shipwreck before looters get there. *Win 5 points.*

An octopus steals your pencil. *Lose 1 point.*

You find a coin with a date stamped on it. *Win 5 points.*

You find pottery containing spices that give you valuable clues about the kind of food eaten by the ship's crew. **Win 1 point.**

BUNDLES *from the* BOGS

Bogs usually develop in poorly drained places where the climate is cold. The soil there is acidic (uh SIHD ihk) and has little oxygen. This means that plants in the bog do not decay quickly, as they do in many other wet climates. Instead, they turn into a spongy soil called peat (peet). When animals fall into a bog and die, their bodies do not decay either. Neither do other natural materials that would normally break up in water. The United States has bogs in Alaska, Florida, Maine, Massachusetts, and Minnesota. But archaeologists have studied some pretty interesting bundles found in bogs in northern Europe, especially in the United Kingdom and Scandinavia.

WHAT IN THE WORLD ARE BOGS?

BOGS ARE WETLANDS, LIKE MARSHES— PART LAND AND PART WATER.

Walk the plank! The ground in a bog is waterlogged, so it is soft. How do archaeologists excavate a bog without crushing the artifacts below with every step? First, they carefully lay wooden planks over the site. Then they stand or kneel on the sturdy planks while they dig.

So what exactly are these bundles? Remember how we said that the bodies of animals do not decay in bogs? Well, the bodies of dead people do not decay either. Archaeologists have found 2,000- to 3,000-year-old bodies that still have hair and skin.

That is a bit yucky, but it is still pretty interesting. People have been finding human mummies in bogs for more than 200 years! One body was discovered in a bog in Denmark in the 1770's, about the time of the American Revolution. Over the centuries, hundreds of bodies have been discovered in bogs in Denmark, Germany, Ireland, the Netherlands, and the United Kingdom.

Human bodies found in bogs are very important. By studying these bodies and artifacts found with them, researchers have discovered important things about people who lived up to 2,000 years ago. We have learned how tall they were. We know what their hair looked like. We know what they wore and what they ate.

For example, about 2,000 years ago, a Roman historian named Tacitus (TAS ih tuhs) described the Germans of his time. He said that the men in a group called the Swabians wore their long hair tied up in a knot. Many years later, a skull found in a German bog still had its hair, even though the flesh and skin were gone. The hair was long and tied up on the skull in a knot. Now we know what Tacitus meant by a "Swabian knot"!

You may be wondering if archaeologists have found clothes from long ago, too. Yes, they have!

This 2,000-year-old skull was found in a bog with its hairdo intact! Swabian men wore their long hair tied up in a knot like the one shown here.

Archaeologists have discovered capes, stockings, and shoes with some bodies. They have also found hundreds of bronze rings, pins, tools, and weapons.

The stomach and intestines of a mummy can be preserved very well in bogs. From these organs, archaeologists can learn something about what people ate thousands of years ago, and they can figure out what animals and plants lived in an area. In the stomach of one bog mummy, scientists found the remains of a kind of porridge called gruel (GROO uhl). It was made of barley and of seeds that were probably gathered in wintertime. Archaeologists also studied the food left in the body of a man called Lindow Man, who had been murdered. They found that he had eaten a piece of burned flat bread that contained some pollen from the mistletoe (MIHS uhl TOH) plant. This kind of bread was used as a magical potion during Lindow Man's time. Some researchers believe that he may have been killed as a sacrifice to the gods.

FEATURED ATTRACTION...

People use the peat from bogs for many things. Gardeners use peat to help their gardens grow. For hundreds of years, people have used peat as fuel to heat their houses. Some people use peat to create electricity. And sometimes people find something besides peat in a bog!

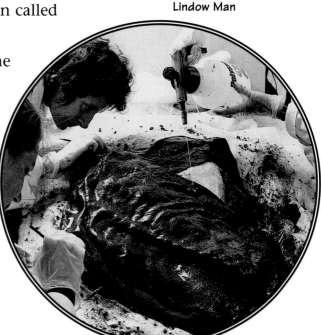

Scientists examining Lindow Man

A CONSERVATOR at WORK

SO WHAT DOES DAN'S MOM DO AT THE MUSEUM?

SHE IS A CONSERVATOR. SHE HELPS PRESERVE AND RESTORE THE ARTIFACTS ARCHAEOLOGISTS FIND.

Have you ever looked in your grandparents' attic? You might find a doll that belonged to your grandmother or a letter that your grandfather wrote. But these things no longer look the way they did when they were new. The doll might be broken or its clothes torn. The paper of the letter may have turned yellow. The ink may be fading.

The things people make do not last forever. Archaeologists do not expect their finds to look new. Colors fade. Metal rusts. Pottery gets

broken. And cloth rots away until only little bits are left. Many objects have survived only because they were underground or underwater. When archaeologists dig them up or bring them to the surface, they decay even faster, sometimes within hours. As a result, efforts to preserve artifacts often begin at the site where the objects are found. Let's say archaeologists bring up a wooden object from the ocean. They would soak it in fresh water immediately to remove the salt.

Most work to preserve artifacts takes place in laboratories or museums. Conservators try to stop old objects from breaking or crumbling any more. They begin by stabilizing (STAY buh lyz ing) the object. For example, that wooden object from the sea is kept in water until it can be treated with a wax or chemicals that replace the water in the cells of the wood. This helps the object keep its original size and shape.

After excavating this dugout canoe, workers found that erosion and insects had severely weakened the wood. Conservators made the cradling frame shown above to support the fragile structure during conservation.

It is important to keep such fragile wood wet at all times. Below, the canoe soaks in a large vat of preservatives. Depending on the wood and how waterlogged it is, the canoe could soak for up to three years.

Once an object has been stabilized, conservators attempt to make it look like it did originally. This stage is called restoration (REHS tuh RAY shuhn). Pieces of broken pottery or glass often can be fitted together, just like the pieces of a jigsaw puzzle. Crust on metals may be removed with acids. Ancient clothing and other textiles may be mended. Leather may be softened and reshaped.

Reconstructed artifacts rarely look exactly like they did originally. Some conservators attempt to restore an object so perfectly that only an expert can detect their work. Other conservators deliberately make their restoration efforts obvious so that future archaeologists will know exactly which parts of the artifact are original.

This reconstructed vase awaits additional finds. But even with a few pieces missing, archaeologists can learn something about this vase and the people who used it.

Specialists called curators (kyoo RAY tuhrz) organize and oversee restored artifacts after conservators are through with them. Curators work in museums or laboratories for long-term preservation and research. The collections that they oversee are viewed and studied by archaeologists and museum visitors.

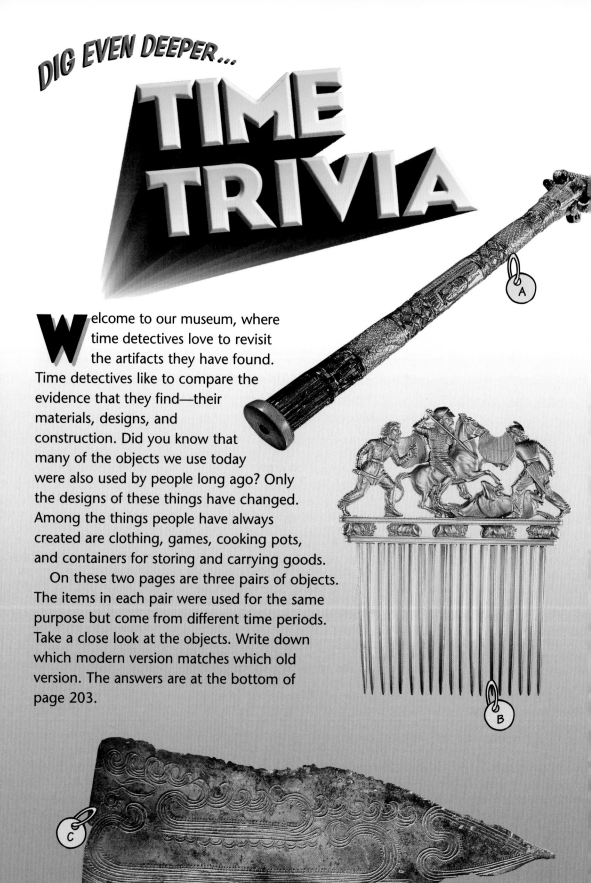

DIG EVEN DEEPER...

TIME TRIVIA

Welcome to our museum, where time detectives love to revisit the artifacts they have found. Time detectives like to compare the evidence that they find—their materials, designs, and construction. Did you know that many of the objects we use today were also used by people long ago? Only the designs of these things have changed. Among the things people have always created are clothing, games, cooking pots, and containers for storing and carrying goods.

On these two pages are three pairs of objects. The items in each pair were used for the same purpose but come from different time periods. Take a close look at the objects. Write down which modern version matches which old version. The answers are at the bottom of page 203.

ANSWERS

(A) A pen holder made of wood and gold from the 1300's B.C. It was discovered in King Tut's tomb.
(E) A plastic marker from the A.D. 2000's. Students around the world use this kind of pen.

(B) A gold ornamental comb from about 300 B.C. It shows Scythian warriors in battle.
(D) A plastic hair clip from the A.D. 2000's.

(C) A Danish razor with designs on it from the late Bronze Age, about 1500 B.C. to 50 B.C.
(F) A disposable plastic razor from the A.D. 2000's.

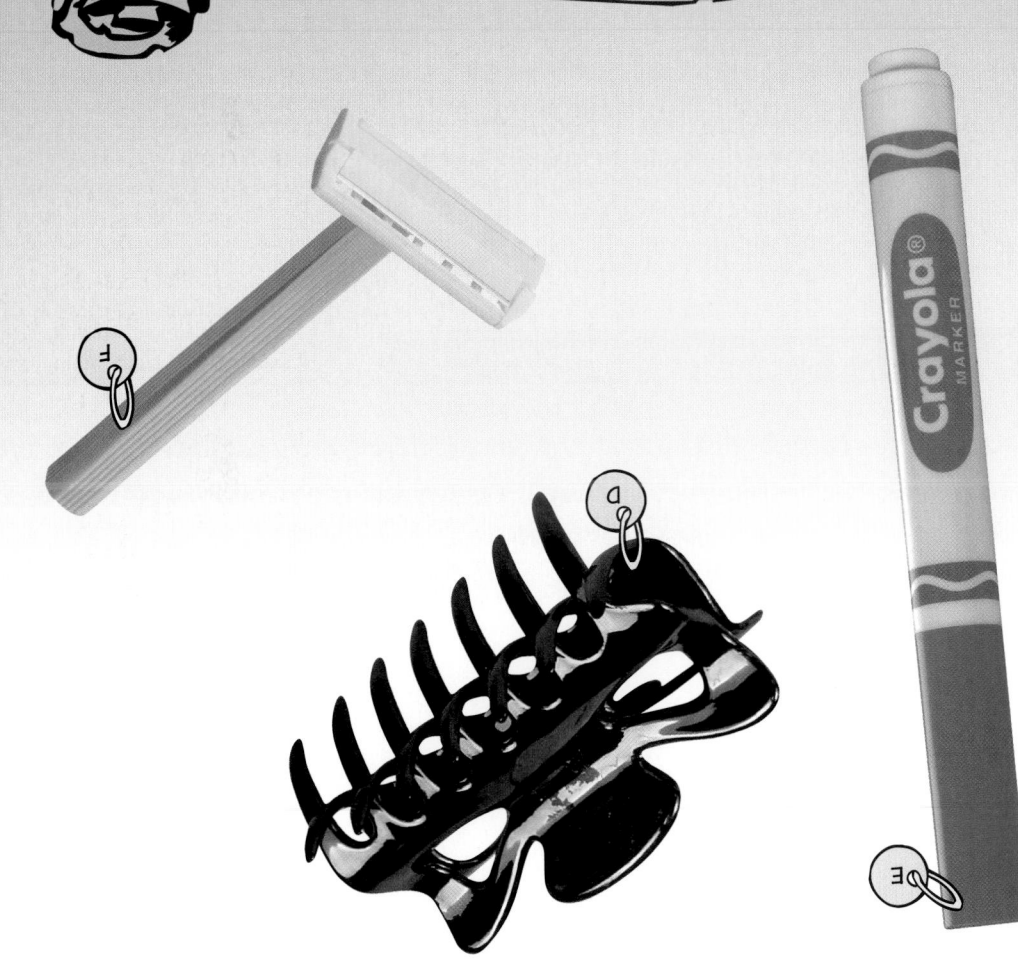

Reconstructing HUMAN FACES

This is what the Yde mummy looked like when it was found. The hair is red, but scientists say that the Yde girl's hair was probably blonde when she was alive. The acid in the bog turned it red.

One day in May 1897, in the Dutch town of Yde, two workers were cutting peat from a bog when they uncovered something bright red. It was a body with red hair! Thinking they had uncovered something devilish, the two workers quickly ran away. Several days later, the town's authorities recovered the body and took it to the Drents Museum in Assen, the Netherlands. Scientists could tell from the bones that the mummy was the remains of a teen-age girl.

The Yde mummy lay in the museum for almost a hundred years. Then in 1992, scientists reexamined the body using new technology. Radiocarbon dating showed that she had died about 2,000 years earlier. X rays of her bones suggested that the girl was about 4 feet 7 inches (142 centimeters) when she died. They also learned about some of her health conditions. But what did this young female look like?

Scientists reconstructed the girl's face using X rays, sculpture, and their knowledge of the structure of the human body.

Based on the mummy's bones, scientists created a sculpture of the Yde girl's head, shown at the right. They inserted pins to represent depths of tissue and to form the nose. Clay was applied to represent muscle.

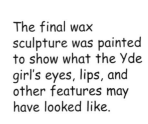

The final wax sculpture was painted to show what the Yde girl's eyes, lips, and other features may have looked like.

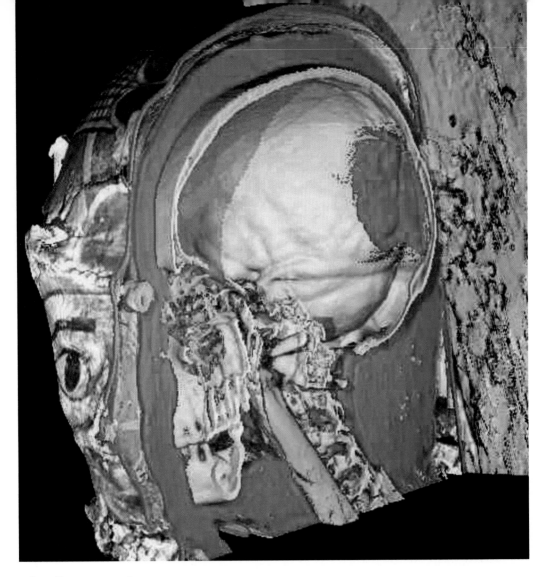

This illustration shows an Egyptian mummy's casing and the skeleton inside. The picture was made using X rays and a computer—and the mummy never had to be unwrapped!

Some mummies are found wrapped and encased, but scientists can reconstruct their faces just as they did for the Yde girl. Scientists take X rays. A computer combines the X rays to show what the mummy looks like on the outside and inside. Scientists can then reconstruct its face without ever unwrapping it. With all these technologies, archaeologists do not only learn about people of the past but also give a face to them as well!

Archaeologist Anna Roosevelt says underwater coastlines, tropical rain forests, and other neglected areas need to be re-examined for clues to our past. Anna is the great-granddaughter of the 26th U.S. President, Theodore Roosevelt. She became interested in archaeology at age 9. She liked reading about archaeology, especially C. W. Ceram's book *Gods, Graves, and Scholars*. Throughout Anna's childhood, her mother took her to many archaeological sites. The discoveries and the excitement stuck with her. She likes following the trail of an idea—digging for days, weeks, months, searching to understand the layers and objects. And she loves the drama and suspense of waiting for the radiocarbon dates to be run. She has made great discoveries, including some in the Amazon tropical rain forest. She also became Curator of Archaeology at the Field Museum in Chicago. Anna loves going to a museum and looking at the artifacts there for more clues. You can, too!

Anna
ROOSEVELT
EXPLORER AND CURATOR

SECRETS *of the* PAST CHRONOLOGY

Archaeologists and other scientists and explorers have unlocked many secrets of the past. Among other discoveries, they found out when ancient cities thrived, when mummies were created, and when toilets first flushed! The approximate dates when those things happened and when many others explored in this book took place are given on this timeline. B.C. is an abbreviation for "before Christ." It is used for dates before the birth of Christ. A.D. is the abbreviation for the Latin words *anno Domini,* meaning "In the year of the Lord." A.D. is used for dates after the birth of Christ. From 100 B.C. to A.D. 100 is 200 years.

B.C.

About 3 million years ago
First stone tools are made.
Africa

About 11,000 B.C.
First pottery is made.
Several areas

About 9000 B.C.
People begin farming.
Asia

About 7000 to 4000 B.C.
Giraffe rock art is made.
Central Sahara

About 4000 B.C.
Rivers begin to dry up.
Sahara

About 5000 to 3000 B.C.
Chinchorro mummies are made.
Chile and Peru

About 5000 B.C.
Bow and arrow are first used.
Egypt

About 7000 B.C.
First known flutes are made.
China

About 3500 to 2000 B.C.
Sumer region thrives; develops cuneiform, the first writing system.
Iraq

About 3500 B.C.
Bronze tools are made.
Asia

About 3500 to 1850 B.C.
City of Ur thrives.
Iraq

About 2000 B.C.
Native American dugout canoes are made.
Florida

About 2500 B.C.
Indus Valley civilization begins to flourish.
Pakistan and India

About 3000 B.C.
First mummies are created.
Egypt

About 3300 B.C.
Ötzi the Iceman dies.
Italy

About 1700 B.C.
Flush toilets are first used.
Crete

About 1500 to 1000 B.C.
Iron tools become popular.
Asia

1339 B.C.
King Tut dies.
Egypt

Late 1300's or 1400's
Last Norse leave their island home.
Greenland

1400's
Gede reaches its height.
Kenya

Mid-1400's
Angkor is abandoned.
Cambodia

About 1500
Juanita is sacrificed.
Peru

Late 1600's and 1700's
African Burial Ground is used.
New York City

1349
Earthquake topples Lighthouse of Alexandria.
Egypt

1000's to 1500's
Novgorod birch-bark letters are written.
Russia

About 985
Norse arrive from Iceland.
Greenland

820 to 1100's
City of Angkor has perhaps a million people.
Cambodia

400's and early 500's
Angles, Saxons, and Jutes invade Britain, and Cadbury Castle is fortified.
Britain

About 500
Early pictographs are made in Sego Canyon.
Utah

600's and 700's
Tikal reaches height of prosperity.
Mexico

250 to 900
Maya civilization thrives.
Central America

100's to 700's
Moche people thrive.
Peru

79
Vesuvius erupts, destroying Pompeii and Herculaneum.
Italy

60
Queen Boadicea attacks Londinium.
Britain

About 196 B.C.
Rosetta stone is carved.
Egypt

First century B.C. or A.D.
Girl dies in Yde bog.
The Netherlands

A.D.

1 to 200
People are buried in the Valley of the Golden Mummies.
Egypt

50 to 100
Lindow Man is sacrificed.
Britain

280 B.C.
Lighthouse at Alexandria is built.
Egypt

450 B.C.
Cat cemetery at Bubastis is popular.
Egypt

About 500 B.C.
Atlai Man dies.
Siberia

600 to 400 B.C.
The Maya build their first large pyramids.
Central America

About 1300 B.C.
Ship sinks at Ulu Burun.
Turkey

1250 or 1184 B.C.
Troy is destroyed.
Turkey

1200 to 400 B.C.
Olmec civilization thrives.
Mexico

About 1000 B.C.
Cherchen Man and Woman die.
China

600's B.C.
First coins are minted.
Turkey

SECRETS of the PAST WORLD MAP

Archaeologists and other scientists and explorers have unlocked many secrets of the past. Among other discoveries, they have found ancient cities in jungles and underwater; mummies in mountains, bogs, and deserts; shipwrecks; rock art; and even love letters written on birch bark! This map shows where some of the discoveries presented in this book were found around the world. Turn to the page numbers listed to find out more about them.

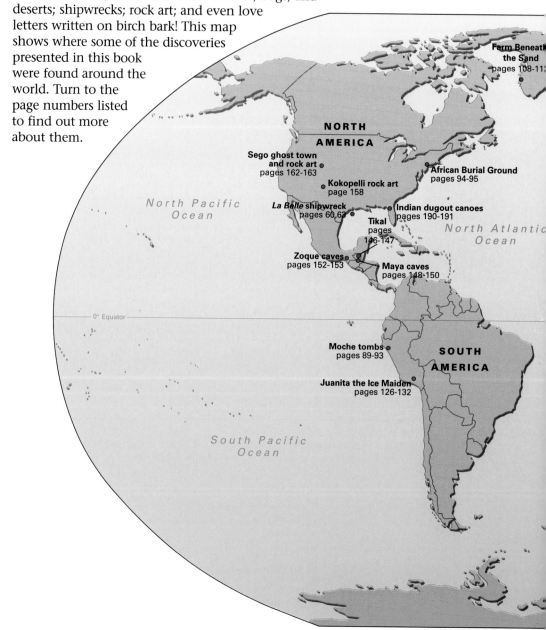

Farm Beneath the Sand
pages 108-11?

NORTH AMERICA

Sego ghost town and rock art
pages 162-163

African Burial Ground
pages 94-95

Kokopelli rock art
page 158

North Pacific Ocean

La Belle shipwreck
pages 60,63

Indian dugout canoes
pages 190-191

Tikal
pages 146-147

North Atlantic Ocean

Zoque caves
pages 152-153

Maya caves
pages 148-150

0° Equator

Moche tombs
pages 89-93

SOUTH AMERICA

Juanita the Ice Maiden
pages 126-132

South Pacific Ocean

Cadbury Castle pages 66-71

London's red layer pages 52-53

Birch-bark letters pages 134-135

Siberian excavation page 132

Altai man page 62

EUROPE

Yde bog girl pages 204-206

Troy page 30

A S I A

Ötzi the Iceman pages 117-123

Ulu Burun shipwreck pages 183-189

Cherchen Man and Woman pages 96-100

Mount Vesuvius pages 38-39

Sumer clay tablet page 165

Chinese flute page 16

Lighthouse of Alexandria pages 174-181

Ur page 17

Valley of the Golden Mummies pages 84-86

Bubastis cat cemetery pages 101-103

Indus Valley civilization page 169

Giraffe rock art page 159

Valley of the Kings pages 74-81

Angkor pages 138-142

AFRICA

North Pacific Ocean

Gede pages 143-145

Indian Ocean

South Atlantic Ocean

Aboriginal rock art of hands page 154

AUSTRALIA

ANTARCTICA

Answer Key

page 109
Norse Riddle
The answer to the riddle is *Viking*.

pages 124-125
Hidden Artifacts
The Ötzi-related artifacts hidden in the tattoo are:
  a carved bow
  two flint-tipped arrows
  two deerskin shoes
  a copper ax
  a grass cape
  a stone knife
The red outlines in this illustration show where you can find the items in the tattoo.

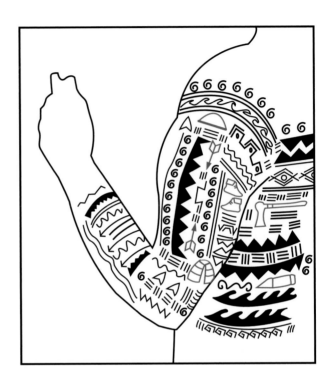

pages 146-147
Hidden in the Jungle
Thank you! You helped uncover the Temple of the Giant Jaguar at Tikal in Guatemala. There is a long stairway up the side of the temple, which is 150 feet (45 meters) tall. Tikal was a city of tens of thousands of people in the A.D. 600's and 700's. Like the ancient Egyptians, the Maya built pyramids to protect the bodies of their buried kings.

FIND OUT MORE

There are so many exciting resources for you to use to learn all about archaeology. You will find plenty to enjoy. The resources listed here are only a sampling. Your school or public library has many more.

For Ages 5-8

Archaeologists Dig for Clues
by Kate Duke (HarperCollins, 1997)

This introduction to archaeology is from the *Let's-Read-and-Find-Out* series for early readers. The author explains what scientists look for, how they find it, and how these clues help them imagine what life was like thousands of years ago.

Mummies and Pyramids: A Nonfiction Companion to Mummies in the Morning
by Will and Mary Pope Osborne (Random House, 2001)

From the popular *Magic Tree House* series, this book provides young readers with answers to many of their questions about pyramids, mummies, hieroglyphics, and much more. Do you know who discovered King Tut's tomb?

Right Here on This Spot
by Sharon Hart Addy (Houghton Mifflin, 1999)

This picture book tells the story of the many users over time of a piece of land. As Grandpa digs a ditch, the discovery of an arrowhead and a Union soldier's button provides evidence of previous occupants.

A Street Through Time
by Anne Millard (DK Publishing, 1998)

In this beautifully illustrated picture book, you will see how a street has changed over 12,000 years. Statues, buildings, and other items have been unearthed and now tell the story of the past.

For Ages 9 and Up

Archaeology for Kids: Uncovering the Mysteries of the Past
by Richard Panchyk (Review Press, 2001)

Combining history and science, this book includes twenty-five fun activities that bring past civilizations to life for children. You will learn to make some of the "tools" that archaeologists use.

Digging to the Past: Excavations in Ancient Lands
by W. John Hackwell (Macmillan, 1986)

Learn the roles of the members of various technical teams of a typical dig, the daily routine of the dig participants, and the steps to the slow uncovering of the homes, artifacts, and tombs of a lost civilization.

Dig's State-by-State Guide to Archaeology and Paleontology Events for Kids, Families and Schools
Web site at http://www.digonsite.com/guide/index.html

This compilation of events, programs, camps, museum exhibits, and educational activities is a good starting point for family outings and field trips related to archaeology. Pick your state of choice and find out what's going on in the world of archaeology!

Egyptian Mummies: The British Museum
by Delia Pemberton (Harcourt, Brace, 2001)

Examination of the remains of seven mummies from the British Museum has unearthed the past. This volume is packed with color photos that show the similarities and differences between Egypt of long ago and Egypt of today.

Exploring for Shipwrecks
by K. C. Smith (Watt, 2000)

This book will answer many of your questions about shipwrecks, including where you would look for one and what tools and techniques you would use to find and study submerged ships.

Ghost Towns of the American West
by Raymond Bial (Houghton Mifflin, 2001)

Through photos and text, the author explains ghost towns as settlements that have been abandoned by all or most of its inhabitants. What is left behind tells the story of previous inhabitants and their way of life.

Ice Maiden of the Andes
by Janet Buell (Twenty-First Century Books, 1997)

Our understanding of the ancient South American civilization of the Inca increased with the discovery of the 500-year-old frozen body of a young girl on a mountaintop in the Andes. The author brings the story of "Juanita" to life for young readers.

Mummies, Bones and Body Parts
by Charlotte Wilcox (Carolrhoda Books, Inc, 2000)

Life in the past can be better understood as a result of scientists' study of mummies' bones and body parts. This author records fascinating stories of human remains.

National Geographic Outpost
Web site at
http://www.nationalgeographic.com/outpost

This interactive Web site allows K-12 students to participate in an expedition with scientists and explorers in the field and ask questions via e-mail. A "tool kit" for each expedition leads users to other links, books, articles, and classroom ideas.

Shipwreck
by Richard Platt (Alfred A. Knopf, 1997)

This well-illustrated volume from the *Eyewitness* series describes the history of shipwrecks and discusses famous wrecks, causes, and rescue techniques. You will also find information on underwater archaeology and the exploration of wrecks.

You Wouldn't Want to Be an Egyptian Mummy
Web site at
http://www.salariya.com/web_books/mummy/

Based on the book by the same title, this Web book allows you to travel to the afterlife. By clicking on images, you can take yourself back 3,000 years and experience the expensive and complicated process of becoming a mummy.

The Young Oxford Book of Archaeology
by Norah Moloney
(Oxford University Press, 1997)

With vivid photos and text, this book takes you on a journey through time. You will learn about archaeology on land and underwater. You will also learn about the Garbage Project, which is a way for modern-day archaeologists to learn more about our own society.

GLOSSARY

Here are some words you have read in this book. The pronunciation given in parentheses after each word tells you how to say it: **acupuncture** (AK yuh PUHNGK chuhr). Say the parts in small letters in your normal voice, those in small capital letters a little louder, and those in large capital letters loudest. Following the pronunciation are one or two sentences that tell the word's meaning as it is used in this book.

acupuncture (AK yuh PUHNGK chuhr)
A form of medical treatment in which very fine needles are inserted into the skin at certain points.

anatomy (uh NAT uh mee)
The science of how a human is structured or put together.

ancestors (AN sehs tuhrz)
Those people from whom one is directly descended. Your grandparents and great-grandparents are your ancestors.

archaeologists
(AHR kee AHL uh jihsts)
Scientists who study people, life, and customs of ancient times.

artifacts (AHR tuh faktz)
Objects that were made, used, or changed by people. Arrowheads and pottery are examples of artifacts.

auger (AW guhr)
A tool in the shape of a long hollow tube that is used to take samples of soil.

bog (bawg)
A type of wetland in which the soil is acidic and lacking in oxygen. These conditions slow the decay of plant and animal matter. The partially decayed organic matter forms a soft, spongy layer of peat.

civilizations (SIHV uh luh ZAY shuhnz)
Societies that are highly developed, especially in their systems of government, trade, agriculture, and the arts and sciences.

conquistadors (kon KEES tuh dawrz)
Spanish conquerors in North and South America, especially during the 1500's.

conservator (KAHN suhr VAY tuhr)
A scientist who helps preserve and restore the artifacts that archaeologists find.

context (KAHN tehkst)
How artifacts and ecofacts were originally placed or found.

corrode (kuh ROHD)
To wear away or eat away gradually. Corrosion is caused by a chemical reaction.

cowrie (KAHW ree) **shells**
The brightly colored, smooth shell of a tropical mollusk. The cowrie shell was used as money in some places and as decoration in other places.

crypt (krihpt)
An underground room or vault.
The crypt beneath the main floor
of a church was formerly often used
as a burial place.

culture (KUHL chuhr)
A certain way of life a group of people
chooses, including their customs and
their arts.

cuneiform (kyoo NEE uh fawrm)
A system of writing used by the people
of ancient Middle Eastern civilizations. Its
characters are made up of small wedges.
The characters were made with a
wedge-shaped tool called a stylus.

curators (kyoo RAY tuhrz)
People who organize and protect
restored artifacts so that others can
enjoy and study them.

decay (dih KAY)
To rot. Organic artifacts decay slowly
over time. Organisms called bacteria and
fungus speed the rate of decay.
Inorganic artifacts do not decay.

decipher (dih SY fer)
To figure out the meaning of something
that is not clear, such as ancient
writings.

demotic (dih MAHT ihk)
A simplified form of ancient Egyptian
writing.

DNA (dee ehn ay)
A chemical found in the nucleus (center)
of all living cells. DNA helps pass
characteristics from one generation to
another. It stands for deoxyribonucleic
(dee ahk suh RY boh noo KLEE ihk) acid.

ecofacts (EE koh FAKTS)
Natural objects that are found with
artifacts at an archaeological site.
Ecofacts, such as seeds and animal
bones, tell us about ancient people's
surroundings and how they lived in
their surroundings.

embalming (ehm BAHM ihng)
The process of treating a dead body
with chemicals and letting it dry to
preserve it.

epigraphers (ih PIHG ruh fuhrz)
People who are skilled in reading
inscriptions, especially those written on
rock, stone, or metal in ancient times.

eruption (ih RUHP shuhn)
The act of exploding or bursting out.
Gases, ash, cinders, or lava may burst
from a volcano during an eruption.

exhibit (ehg ZIHB iht)
A display of objects for the public.
Information about the objects is usually
included in the exhibit.

geology (jee AHL uh jee)
The study of the earth's history through
its soil and rocks, including how they
have changed and how they are
changing.

hieroglyphics (HY uhr uh GLIHF ihks)
A system of pictures, characters, or
symbols used for writing. Each picture or
symbol, called a hieroglyph, stands for a
certain word, idea, or sound. The
ancient Egyptians used hieroglyphics
rather than an alphabet.

hypothesis (hy PAHTH uh sihs)
An educated guess.

inhabitants (ihn HAB uh tuhnts)
The people or animals that live in a
place.

limestone (LYM stohn)
A kind of soft rock that can be carved
easily.

magnetometer (MAG nuh TAHM uh
tuhr)
An instrument used to find certain buried
objects, such as those made of iron.

midden (MIHD duhn)
A mound of food waste and trash.
When archaeologists dig up middens
of prehistoric peoples, they find many
artifacts and ecofacts that give them
clues about how ancient people lived.

mosque (mahsk)
A place of worship for Muslims.

mummify (MUHM uh fy)
A process used to prevent dead
bodies from decaying. Sometimes
extremely cold or dry conditions
naturally mummify a dead body.

mummy (MUHM ee)
A dead body that has been preserved
and contains some of the body's soft
tissues. Some mummies are found
wrapped and in decorated coffins.

organic (awr GAN ihk)
Something that comes from a plant
or animal. Wooden objects are organic.
The wood was once part of a living tree.
Leather is organic. It comes from
animal hides.

papyrus (puh PY ruhs)
A tall plant that the ancient Egyptians,
Greeks, and Romans used to make a kind
of paper. They used the paper for writing
messages and in making masks for
mummies.

peat (peet)
A kind of heavy, spongy soil that
is made from partly rotten moss and
other organic materials.

petroglyphs (PEHT ruh glihfs)
Pictures that are engraved into a rock.

pharaoh (FAIR oh)
The title given to the kings of ancient
Egypt.

pictographs (PIHK tuh grafs)
Pictures that are painted onto a rock.
Before the alphabet was developed,
ancient peoples sometimes shared
information using pictographs.

pigment (PIHG muhnt)
A coloring matter, usually a powder or
a substance that can be easily crushed.
Adding pigment to oil, water, or some
other liquid material makes paint.

pottery (PAHT uhr ee)
Pots, dishes, vases, and similar objects
that are made from clay and hardened
by heat. Bits of pottery are called shards.

prehistoric (PREE hihs TAWR ihk)
The time before people began to
write down information.

preservative (prih ZUR vuh tihv)
A substance that is used to prevent
decay. Salt is a preservative.

privy (PRIHV ee)
A small outhouse used as a toilet
and often as a place to throw out
garbage. The contents of a privy help
archaeologists find out what people
ate and drank, what diseases they had,
and what medicine they took.

radiocarbon (RAY dee oh KAHR buhn)
A radioactive form of carbon found in
all living things. Archaeologists can
determine how old some organic objects
are by measuring the amount of
radioactive carbon they contain.

restoration (REHS tuh RAY shuhn)
Making an object look the way it did
originally.

sarcophagus (sahr KAHF uh guhs)
A stone coffin. It is believed that the
ancient Egyptians made the first of these
stone coffins for the burial of a king or
famous person.

screen (skreen)
A tool that has many small holes in
the bottom of it. It is used to sift dirt to
find artifacts. It lets through very small
pieces of dirt but holds back larger ones.
It is also known as a sieve.

scribes (skrybz)
People who were trained to write letters
or books by hand for others. Before
printing was invented, there were many
scribes.

scuba (SKOO buh)
Portable breathing equipment used by
underwater swimmers and divers.

shamans (SHAH muhnz)
Priests or healers with magic powers over diseases or evil spirits.

shards (shahrdz)
Bits and pieces of clay vases, jars, pitchers, plates, or other pottery. Archaeologists often find many shards when they excavate a site, because shards do not decay. Shards are also called sherds or potsherds.

sieve (sihv)
A tool that has many small holes in the bottom of it. It is used to sift dirt to find artifacts. It lets through very small dirt particles but holds back larger ones. It is also known as a screen.

silt (sihlt)
Small pieces of dirt and other matter that are carried along by flowing water. Silt sometimes covers and preserves artifacts.

site (syt)
A place where archaeologists choose to excavate. It is also called an excavation site.

sonar (SOH nahr)
A tool used for detecting and locating objects underwater by the reflection of sound waves.

sphinx (sfihngks)
An imaginary creature of ancient myths. The sphinx most often had the body of a lion and the head of a human, ram, or falcon. Some also had wings and a serpent's tail.

stabilizing (STAY buh lyz ihng)
Making an object firm to stop it from breaking, crumbling, or decaying.

statue (STACH yoo)
An image of a person or animal carved from wood or stone or made from metal, clay, or wax.

stelae (STEE lee)
Large stones that have inscriptions or sculptured designs. In ancient Greece and Rome, stelae were used to mark graves.

stratigraphy (struh TIHG ruh fee)
Using the arrangement and layers of rocks and artifacts to determine the age and history of a site. The layers of a site are called strata.

stylus (STY luhs)
A tool used for writing. A wedge-shaped stylus was used to inscribe cuneiform on metal, stone, or wet clay. A sharp, pointed stylus was used to write on wax or wax-like surfaces.

submersibles (suhb MUR suh buhlz)
Boats or ships used underwater to explore the ocean.

sundial (SUHN DY uhl)
An instrument that tells the time of the day by the position of a shadow cast by the sun.

survey (suhr VAY)
To search an area for archaeological evidence.

Swahili (swah HEE lee)
An African language that uses many Arabic and other foreign words.

tattoo (ta TOO)
A picture, design, or motto that has been put on the skin by pricking a line of holes and putting in colors.

tells (tehlz)
Mounds that form on a landscape as people build over older sites again and again in the same area over a long period of time.

textile (TEHKS tuhl)
A woven fabric or cloth.

theory (THEE uhr ee)
An explanation based on observation and reasoning. Archaeologists create theories about people of the past. The theories are based partly on the artifacts they find.

Titanic (ty TAN ihk)
A British ship that struck an iceberg and sank on its first trip from England to New York City in April 1912.

INDEX

This index is an alphabetical list of important topics covered in this book. It will help you find information given in both words and pictures. To help you understand what an entry means, there is sometimes a helping word in parentheses, for example, **Alexandria** (city). If there is information in both words and pictures, you will see the words *with pictures* in parentheses after the page number. If there is only a picture, you will see the word *picture* in parentheses after the page number.

ILLUSTRATION ACKNOWLEDGMENTS

The publishers of Childcraft gratefully acknowledge the courtesy of the following photographers, agencies, and organizations for the photographs and illustrations in this volume. When all the illustrations for a sequence of pages are from a single source, the inclusive page numbers are given. Credits should be read from left to right, top to bottom, on their respective pages. All illustrations are the exclusive property of the publisher of Childcraft unless names are marked with an asterisk (*).

Covers:
Aristocrat, Discovery, International, and Standard Bindings—illustration by Paul Perreault
Heritage Binding—Meredith Johnson; © David Muench*; Tom Herzberg; Tom Herzberg; Paul Perrault; Meredith Johnson; J. Delafosse, Discovery Channel* Janice Skivington; Paul Perrault

Rainbow Binding—© David R. Frazier*; Meredith Johnson; © Boltin Picture Library*

10-11   Paul Perrault
12-13   Tom Herzberg; Meredith Johnson; Tom Herzberg
14-15   Tom Herzberg; © Gianni Dagli Orti, Corbis*; © Carl Hansen*
16-17   Tom Herzberg; © Garman Harbottle, Juzhong Zhang,

Changsui Wang, and Zhaochen Kong*; © Ronald Sheridan, Ancient Art & Architecture Collection Ltd.*

18-19   Paul Perrault; © Chris Hellier, Ancient Art & Architecture Collection Ltd.*; P. S. Martin*
20-21   Tom Herzberg
22-23   © Ronald Sheridan, Ancient Art & Architecture Collection Ltd.*; Tom Herzberg